DANCING WITH WELK

DANCING WITH WELK

MUSIC, MEMORY, AND
PRAIRIE TROUBADOURS

CHRISTOPHER VONDRACEK

SOUTH DAKOTA HISTORICAL SOCIETY PRESS

PIERRE

Printed in the United States of America

Library of Congress Cataloging-in-Publication Data
Names: Vondracek, Christopher, author.
Title: Dancing with Welk : music, memory, and prairie troubadours / by Christopher Vondracek.
Description: Pierre: South Dakota Historical Society Press, 2022.
Identifiers: LCCN 2022004617 (print) | LCCN 2022004618 (ebook) | ISBN 9781941813416 (paperback) | ISBN 9781941813423 (epub)
Subjects: LCSH: Welk, Lawrence, 1903-1992. | Vondracek, Christopher. | Musicians—North Dakota. | Musicians—South Dakota.
Classification: LCC ML422.W33 V66 2022 (print) | LCC ML422.W33 (ebook) | DDC 780.0978—dc23
LC record available at https://lccn.loc.gov/2022004617
LC ebook record available at https://lccn.loc.gov/2022004618
The paper in this book meets the guidelines for permanence and durability of the Committee on Production Guidelines for Book Longevity of the Council on Library Resources.

Please visit our website at sdhspress.com

26 25 24 23 22   1 2 3 4 5

Cover images: helenreveur/Shutterstock (accordion); paseven/Shutterstock (background)

Cover and book design by Mayfly Design

For my grandparents

"Two-step—it's all they're dancing nowadays. The waltz is through."

—Richard Rodgers, *Oklahoma*

"'We were up there drinking beer where Lawrence Welk used to sit,' Jerry Garcia says.

The little girl who was dancing by herself giggles. 'Too much,' she says softly. Her eyes are still closed."

—Joan Didion, *The White Album*

"Vainly I had sought to borrow | From my books surcease of sorrow."

—Edgar Allan Poe, "The Raven"

CONTENTS

DANCE #3: A SCHOTTISCHE

THE BAND IS WARMING UP . . .

The Dakotas once boasted tens of thousands of accordionists. Every barn dance on the county line featured a gleeful, bow-legged farm boy pumping a squeezebox, spraying notes in the air like birds, flooding the sky from a barren cottonwood at a passing car's backfiring. The banker, the church deacon, the schoolteachers hiding flasks, and pretty girls with curly hair and soda pop smiles weaved in figure eights, while young men huddled amongst themselves chewing on straw. But up on the hay bale stood the vested musician. He stomped his feet into the beat while the navy sky above the roof of the barn, festooned in chrysanthemums, grew darker and darker still.

I am told America was young then.

Towns painted "Come for an Afternoon, Stay for a Lifetime" on the side of the brick pharmacy. Choirs sang in the park in gazebos on lazy Saturdays. America swelled full of hope. Dances tore through town like festive little twisters, pulling in people, the town dog, a few drunks, and by morning, the mysterious boy with the accordion had been spun far out of town, too, as hangdog strangers stood by the pharmacy pulling on their faces, saying, *my, that kid could play, could fly*.

But that is all gone now.

America is very old today. Recent accounts put the number of accordionists residing in the Dakotas closer to 317. The *New York Times* just reported the last accordion repairman closing up shop in Manhattan. I've lived most my life between the Mississippi and Missouri rivers and only once attended a barn dance. It was actually inside a steel shed. There was no hay.

But accordions are still lying around—like fossilized femurs sticking up out of a farmer's bean field, discovered just before spring planting.

Many years ago, I went to a friend's house. She had an accordion in her closet. "A few keys are stuck," Abigail told me, sadly.

Abigail was making her way in the theater. The instrument resting in her lap had belonged to her German grandparents. As her dark hair cascaded over her blue eyes, she whispered, "But it could give me an edge at auditions."

I didn't have the heart to tell Abigail that now is no longer the time for accordions. Most of America's great squeezeboxers—Frankie Yankovic, Myron Floren, and Lawrence Welk—are goners. All that's left is Gogol Bordello and "Weird Al" Yankovic, a curly-haired parodist who rose to fame after changing the lyrics of the Knack's 1979 hit to "My Bologna."

The accordion is a simple instrument—a bellows squeezing air through crude pipes, opened or closed by the key-stop you push. Some instruments last longer than others. The guitar. The piano. The National Music Museum in Vermillion, South Dakota, houses a collection of instruments that didn't make the cut like the serpent (an early saxophone) and the two-belled euphonium. There's even an accordion from Paris, circa 1830.

It resembles an unfolded book.

I once led a band, the Brickhouse Boys, who tried to get famous from the middle of nowhere. One night, we even played the World's Only Corn Palace. On a flatbed trailer stretching beneath the yellow onion domes, our singer, Bobby, in snakeskin boots, keened a melody to the crowd from his knees. His older brother, Donny, dropped a few pheasants dead from the sky with the craaaaack of his snare drum. Over near the caramel-corn stirrer, our fedora-clad guitarist, Poncho, bobbed up and down like a latter-day wizard, coaxing electric life from the theremin. Monster (who had run for mayor of Rapid City at eighteen years old) ran through the street with a tambourine, while my nineteen-year-old kid brother, Leo, our bassist, who had won our town's talent show for singing "Blue Moon" three years prior, thumbed a moody, scarecrow groove.

Oh, and there was me. I played piano. Under the yellow wall of that agrarian cathedral, my jangling piano and the sound of all of us together, like busted window panes from old farmhouse windows shot out by barnstorming teenagers, ricocheted off downtown Mitchell's buildings, carrying our great whirl of music, our Roman candle of squeezed-up, fingers-clenched ambition exploding into the night, audible to the nearby fields, towns, and heavy-eyed interstate truckers.

We would never reach the magnitude of Lawrence Welk, undoubtedly the most famous musician to emerge from the Dakotas, whose golden-bulb marquee lit the brightest on dark prairie nights, whose name still tumbled out of dairy cooperative trucks when parked under a mural in Irene, South Dakota, who echoed in the ears of a mustachioed man shuffling a crate into a gas station and spotting an old dance partner running the till.

When my wife, Carrie, was just my girlfriend, we visited Lu Ella Machin, age eighty-five, who had laid out polka paraphernalia on a card table next to the *TIME* magazines, and welcomed us into her senior-living apartment in Yankton to tell us what she knew about Lawrence Welk.

"Lawrence was a PANcordion man," she said. "Lou was Italo-American out of Chicago."

Lu Ella's husband, Lou Prohut, had a competing television show on ABC called *Polka-Go-Round*. Among accordionists, Lou was a real ham, flying across glistening ballroom floors, his dexterous fingers crab walking up and down the keyboard.

"You know, that accordion factory smelled like honey," Lu Ella said. "They used beeswax as adhesive."

I nodded. The interview, set up by Carrie's father, a hip and knee surgeon, was okay. But not great. As much as I admired the man's gumption and transportational prowess, I hadn't come down here for stories of Lou "Flying Fingers" Prohut.

"So you said you hung out in Lawrence's trailer?" asked Carrie.

At reference to his name, Lu Ella's eyes—quick as jackrabbits—narrowed in on me.

"Well, yes."

"So, like, how was he? Funny? Smart?" Carrie asked.

Carrie had worked for a senator in Washington, D.C., for many years and was more probing with her questions than me, even though I was technically a journalist.

Lu Ella leaned back in her chair, her white bob of hair cascading down to her shoulder. Suddenly, she snapped forward.

"Well, he ate baby food," Lu Ella said. "How about that?"

"Welk ate baby food straight from the jar."

History, anymore, comes to me mostly in gossip or objects left behind—like finding an old microwave buried in a field—by which you can say, "these people were like me, too."

But I don't trust the stories of the dead.

Unless they're the ones talking.

West of Hague, North Dakota, there is a cemetery with metallic, Ukrainian-style crosses erected by Welk's blacksmith father, Ludwig. In five hundred years, the son's music will have faded, but these stark and bizarre crosses in the prairie grass might still be there, and future generations will curiously wonder about their anonymous, master craftsman, this artist, who imbued into steel sublime symphonies of emotion, music into metal.

Are we to comfort or challenge those in our time, or those for a future time? I don't know. But dedication to the living or those who *will* be living is not the only way to think about an artist's task. Sometimes, maybe like Ludwig, it's okay to think about our dead and how our work can become a small monument to them, lasting long after the wind and rain and snow have chipped away and transformed the last physical thing.

Which brings us to this book in your hand.

Think of it as sheet music to a song I started singing long ago.

So many people say America is in decline. That our great Lawrence Welk Empire is behind us. But don't be fooled. Our past is nostalgic mishmash and roadside junk hawked on cable television shows.

Once a kid who'd heard I was writing a book on Lawrence Welk and this forgotten time told me he had a joke.

"Did you hear why *The Lawrence Welk Show* had to go off the air?" he asked.

"No," I said. "I have not."

He grinned madly, his stocking cap squeezing his red face in the cold air.

"Yeah, I guess, the censors said there was too much sax and violins."

Christopher Vondracek, July 4, 2021

Three Dances for a Nickel . . .

DANCE #1

A POLKA

CHAPTER 1

A BOOKSTORE IN CHARLOTTESVILLE, VIRGINIA

FEBRUARY 9, 2019

I regretted walking into the little bookstore a block off the University of Virginia campus—one of these stuffy places with tiny spectacles and wrinkled noses, the smell of expensive Italian roast coffee and refined taste in the air—when I overheard a conversation.

"Oh, Vincent Price was quite the gourmet. Did you know that?"

"I saw Vincent Price at a Chicken Delight in New York City—do you remember those?"

Naturally, I shrank under the hovering cloud of refinement. "Gourmet" is not a word used in my rural hometown, unless as an adjective for fancy mustards. Moreover, it's an emotional crime, albeit a minor one, when your love of a song or a book is made to feel rotten by someone who'd just as soon blow out your candle anyway.

Nevertheless, I sniffed around the paperback fiction, trying to block out the confab between the grey-haired merchant and a patron jangling a glowing moonstone keychain, when a thread of the conversation slipped in uninvited.

"There was this bookstore owner in Augustine," said the owner's husband, scribbling out notes, "Or maybe Petersburg? Florida, anyway. And he ordered one thousand copies of that man's book. Can you believe it?"

"Oh, he was so schmaltzy," giggled the patron, "So ersatz."

"Yes, he was," the patron's husband continued. "You've no qualm with me there. But here's the kicker. On opening weekend, he sold out the man's autobiography."

Hiding behind a stack of listless transcendentalists, I raised my ear. Whose biography made such a showing?

"In one weekend," the owner remarked. "A thousand copies."

"He knew his audience, certainly," breathlessly replied the husband, rummaging to the back with a box of warped, dog-eared travelogues.

"Oh yes," the owner said. "*Ah one and ah two.*"

"My God," sputtered the patron. "Who would've guessed?"

Dilatorily, I made my move.

It shouldn't have surprised me to run into him at the base of the Blue Ridge Mountains. Since I picked up his little book at Grandma's back in South Dakota a dozen years earlier, I had seen him on a matted poster above a urinal in the restrooms of the Peabody Hotel in Memphis, in sepia-toned wallpaper outside a theater on the Sunset Strip in Hollywood, and on a pinewood placard stuck up in the heart of Interior, South Dakota, deep in the Badlands, just north of the White River and the Pine Ridge Indian Reservation, noting the town's major events: "The great Jim Thorpe has played my fields. The early music of Lawrence Welk has sounded in my nights."

Even today, you'll still hear his name, the cheesy TV bandleader beamed into the homes of millions of Americans, with parents forcing restless teenagers in cotton turtlenecks to spend an hour on Saturday night watching the man's show with their grandparents at their side before the rabbit-eared television.

He was the Champagne Music Maker.

The Strasburg Svengali.

"Your father's family had a nickname for him," Mom would say, if she were telling this story. "Grandpa called him the Polka Elvis."

The Polka Elvis.

But if I were telling the story, I would call Lawrence Welk our prairie troubadour. The only man from the Dakotas to get famous making music. And, more importantly, he was maybe responsible for my very existence.

Both of my parents watched *The Lawrence Welk Show*. As a kid in the early 1960s, my mom sat with her black bowl cut beneath her older siblings watching the cooing Lennon Sisters on that bunny-eared television up in Beresford, South Dakota. Meanwhile, one hundred miles southwest in Verdigre, Nebraska, my dad similarly lay sprawled on a couch in flannel pajamas with his four siblings, watching those same Lennon Sisters and wondering how children just a few years older than him had made it onto the television they were all looking at.

My respective grandfathers complained. Ed McGill, a grocer with a white shock of hair, groused at Irish Tenor Joe Feeney. "Why not hire a howling Labrador?" he would lament. "The dog would, at least, be less nasally."

My dad's dad, George Jr., a World War II veteran of a hospital boat in the Pacific and then a band director, a husky, bearded man who played tuba for years in the local polka scene, had a different gripe. He knew guys Welk stiffed. "The man pays his musicians scale!" Grandpa would shout. It was the sharpest critique.

Of course, my grandfathers were both flea-bitten with envy. George skulked away in the northeast Nebraska polka circuit, while Ed sang Irish dirges at the funerals in the tri-county, and both knew only one musician could get famous from their backcountry.

But apparently these mutual sentiments about Welk had been so very important for young George III (my father) and Rita (my mother) that when, in the early 1980s, they were the only two single teachers in Hurley, South Dakota—a tiny wink of a stop on the map with one of those rickety, wooden, defeatist signs advertising the number of county football championships won by the local high school—they went out on a date to a musical theater production in Mitchell, home of the World's Only Corn Palace, and struck up a conversation about Welk.

I don't know the exact implications of such a conversation. But we're not a "touchy-feely" family. My brother and I recall seeing our parents kiss only rarely. But I've seen them tell stories about watching *The Lawrence Welk Show*—the laughter over trying to name the singing Oklahoma twins, the escape provided by the revolving door of Champagne Ladies. I knew then that watching them tell these stories—a flip of my mom's hair, my dad's face going flush—was like watching my parents kiss.

So I knew that without Welk, it was quite possible the two teachers from Hurley may have never gone on a second date in 1980, when Welk had already been in syndication for ten years, which means my grandfathers would have never played in a polka band at my parents' wedding reception in 1982, which means by 1984, the year Welk was retired in California as the richest entertainer in Hollywood outside Bob Hope, I may never have been born. As a result, in 1992, the year Welk died of pneumonia, his book *America the Beautiful* would have been checked out for the very last time at the Rochester, Minnesota, public library, because in 2010—three years after I had gone on tour with a band across the less shuttered regions of the Upper Midwest and was researching for a memoir about music on the prairie—I would never have come along and told the librarian to fill up my cart with everything she had in the stacks about that former polka maestro.

My brother Leo once rightly observed that all celebrities must fade. When the world—naturally, justifiably—eulogized the passing of Etta James, Leo pointed out that, it actually would have been stranger, even unnatural, had she not at some point drifted into the beyond to sing for the angels.

Nevertheless, I sometimes wonder if Welk's decline has been particularly undignified. So, on that otherwise ordinary day in the

Charlottesville bookstore, I shuffled around the stack of books into the main thoroughfare of that store and impertinently interjected with what I'd been studying the last decade or so.

"Prentice Hall, 1971," I declared. "That's the publisher and year of that book, *Wunnerful, Wunnerful*. The other four—between us here—would surprise me to have sold like the first."

A look of puzzlement fixed onto the bespectacled faces.

"Is that so?" asked the startled patron, adjusting her translucent frames. "Well, was it any good? The book that is? Was it well-reviewed? Was it companionable?"

And I picked at my collar at the decidedly complicated question.

Certainly, if my interlocutor wanted a book on prairie music, there are better options. Jon Hassler's *Rookery Blues*. Chuck Klosterman's *Fargo Rock City*. Willa Cather's *Song of the Lark* is my favorite.

Wunnerful, Wunnerful was just a hagiographic mishmash: a boy squeezing blindly on a hayloft finds his calling and sets out to conquer America. If you've seen any rock music biopic—*Ray, Walk the Line*, that weird one about Meatloaf—you've seen the setup. At any point you half expect a famous mazurka star to pop into Welk's dreams and whisper the chords to a nickelodeon thumper.

Yet, there are some partisans. I once called up Sherwin Linton, a self-made country star from Watertown, South Dakota, who put out an album in the 1970s titled, I suppose accurately, *I Am Not Johnny Cash*. But I ended up chatting a lot longer with his wife.

"Welk's book is a 'must-read,' for any aspiring musician," she told me.

"Why's that?" I asked.

"Because he . . ."

She ripped open a bag of pretzels.

". . . tells you how he actually did it."

But I didn't say any of that nonsense to the woman in that Virginia bookstore. There was a far more direct reason why I had taken interest in *Wunnerful, Wunnerful*.

"The book is filled with secrets," I told her, brazenly.

She recoiled, eyes bulging, twisting her confoundingly large keychain made of amethyst around her bulbous knuckles.

"My God! What kind of secrets?"

Back in the former Dakota Territory, I had heard all the rumors: about Welk's alleged cheapness, about his fly-by-night escapades, even his pastoral paramours. Not all of them showed up in the book. Sometimes the book had secret-shaped holes. I had come to learn that, too.

"Well," I said, "Once a Sioux City music store owner got on stage at intermission when Welk played the Ritz Ballroom and confiscated his band's instruments because the bandleader hadn't made a down payment."

The woman eyed me with her lids half concealed like waning moons, judging whether she had encountered one of these shyster frauds you hear about who bounce from bookstore to bookstore telling big stories and distributing business cards.

"Hadn't heard that one yet," she replied. "And how do you know?"

I was on my heels now.

The real reason was because my Grandma told me. Delores O'Connor, then a twenty-two-year-old farmer's daughter, stood in back that night at the Ritz, sipping a white-wine spritzer, removing the sawdust from her pumps, eyeing that dropout from Creighton who wanted to be a singer. But I couldn't offer such tepid credibility.

Instead, I aimed higher.

"Because I'm working on a book," I said. "I've fact checked."

"Smashing. I had hoped so," the woman said, her eyebrows starkly raised, trembling suspiciously. "And who is your publisher?"

"Well," I stammered. "I . . ."

And there was the rub. There was no publisher. No one had wanted to publish my book. That had been known for a while. That's why I was here with my wife in a dented-up Prius on a Saturday afternoon and not gallivanting around southern France working on my third novel. No, I had shopped my half-finished manuscript around to various people, including a North Dakotan who worked for a New York publisher, but the comments were always one or the other.

"There's too much Lawrence Welk," or, "Who is Lawrence Welk?"

Nevertheless, I stuck to my guns, learning from Welk to always be a salesman, even in the shortest of meetings.

"No one yet," I told the woman. "But someone someday will read my story."

She smiled at me now, grabbing her copy of the Sunday edition of the *Richmond Times-Dispatch* under her arm, a couple paperback novels.

"Well, I'll look for it," she said, winking. "Maybe it'll sell a thousand copies."

Carrie and I walked onto the cobblestones of Charlottesville. In hours, there was a big basketball game between UVA and Duke. I twirled on the mystery of how Welk's name had traveled even here.

"You know, he was on television for thirty years," I muttered, sheepishly. "He's still on television, even. It's not *that* odd he'd show up here."

Carrie has kept this thing at arm's length. To her, Welk may as well be a stranger sleeping on our back porch who occasionally comes in to use the shower. Perhaps it was the doldrums of a Saturday afternoon setting in or the anticipation of a long drive home, but on this cold day in February, passing by a bar with students in orange sweatshirts hollering at students in blue sweatshirts, Carrie turned to me and asked a question she had never posed to me before.

"How *did* you ever get interested in this whole thing? You know, the Welk stuff?"

I stopped there, two leather shoes snapping together, the cold winter air—even in the American Southland, where the magnolias had not yet bloomed—slicing down my bare throat.

"Have I," I spoke with a lilt, "ever told you about walking to Nebraska?"

"No," my wife said, her big blue eyes, blinking behind her black frames.

"Well, we should start there," I said. "The rest, I hope, will follow."

CHAPTER 2

ON THE ROAD TO NEBRASKA,
SOUTH OF VERMILLION, SOUTH DAKOTA

JUNE 15, 2007

I never considered myself a musician.

Musicians were scoundrels. They got paid with olives in their beer. They traveled vast stretches of uninhabited Nebraska to play postage-stamp bars.

Pianist? Kinda wimpy. Songwriter? Kinda Carole King-y. I preferred to just say I played in a band—and only if someone asked. A musician? No.

But weeks before college graduation, my girlfriend, Heather, set me on her couch and addressed her chief complaint about our nearly year-long relationship.

"I just can't date a musician, Christopher."

"A musician!" I spat.

I played a mean upright piano down at Open Mic's bar in downtown Vermillion on weeknights. But I also lived in a Catholic Church. I wore straight-legged jeans. I wasn't any musician.

"Yeah right, Christopher," Heather said. "I can tell how much you love it."

Panicking, I pleaded mitigating nuances.

"I can play for you at our wedding!" I pleaded. "I can teach our children. Just two more years, honest!"

Heather's blue eyes welled up.

"You promise?"

I nodded.

But I didn't need two years. Two months later, we had broken up and I was tromping toward the Nebraska border.

High above the Missouri River a bridge stretched to Mulberry Outlook, on the Nebraska side, and there, among the dandelions and tall grass, I would walk and view the vast floodplain, the muck and trees and river slatted by sandbars, and maybe figure out what to do with my life.

"Nothing changes!" I shouted.

As I walked, rounding the miniature airport with the old, rusty fighter jet from World War II on stumps, my mind twisted in a kaleidoscope of regrets.

"Nothing changes!" I shouted again. "It all stays the same!"

But no response. Only the *shhhhhhh* of the wind brushing grass whistled.

I am now writing from our home in Washington, D.C., under a painting of Jules Breton's *Song of the Lark,* featured on Willa Cather's novel of the same name. Carrie had it up in our home since I first moved in with her back in Sioux Falls.

The *Song of the Lark* figures a nineteenth-century opera star born on the prairie who takes New York City by storm. I—and maybe you, too—wonder about the dubiousness of such a trajectory. A rural prima donna? Please. The only person who did that was Lawrence Welk. And he was sort of a musical blunderbuss.

Song of the Lark, after all, is really about the economic market of pianos. As people settled the hinterlands, Willa writes, the trains chugged in shiny, black pianos to plop down into tidy prairie homes. Unsurprisingly, people wanted music out here, too.

At least pianos shut up the accordionists and fiddlers.

But *Song of the Lark* is fiction, which is to say, lies. And a musician must contend with real odds. Real musicians can't do what Welk did from the heartland.

I've rounded up some numbers to prove it.

In 1931, during Welk's halcyon days, South Dakota had 694,000 people. By 1984, the year I was born one state to the east in Minnesota, my mother's homeland of South Dakota had grown only by three thousand souls. The Dust Bowl wiped out a generation of folks. America grew, but we just stayed the same out here. Our odds decreased.

A lot of pianos just sat dusty and out of tune. Same with accordions.

There is one line from *Song of the Lark* I think still holds true, however. Willa writes, "Every artist makes himself born."

Walking out from Vermillion that evening, I didn't know it, but I was doing the same.

Making myself born.

A pickup with a gun rack backfired nearby, but I was making myself born.

Or, I prefer, giving myself a name.

Down Dakota Street, I strode in my Converse shoes, moseying through Lower Vermillion, one of these Faulknerian soundstages, with old chicken wire running as a fence and hand-painted "Fresh Produce" signs plotted in front lawns adjacent to wooden signs of blue, polka-dotted dresses bending over, revealing white bloomers, and then I was out of town, toward a cornfield, passing by a backfiring Ford Econoline.

"I'm not a musician!" I called back.

I used to walk along the Vermillion River in those days wondering whether I was a "musician" or a "writer." My mother was a small-town English teacher, my father a band director. Onomatopoeia, as you'll recall from sophomore American Literature, is where language and sound meet. It's a cruder poetics.

The bicycle *buzzed*. The birds *chirped*. The tuba goes *oom-pa-pa*. The man twirling plates atop a ladder falls and goes *splat*. This sort of thing.

Children love onomatopoeia. So did Lawrence Welk's audience.

In an episode of *The Lawrence Welk Show* from 1965, pianist Bob Ralston performs "Poor Butterfly." It's onomatopoeia in reverse. Rather than language imitating sound, it's sound imitating language. His supple hands, like a pair of ragged claws scuttling up and down the floors of silent seas, arpeggiate, arpeggiate, as the silvery wings flap, a delicate arabesque of the poor butterfly stretches herself up toward the chandeliers, toward the hot lights, toward the ceiling, bursting through and flitting into the sky, blue and radiant.

Onomatopoeia can be a maudlin approach to entertainment. But out on the prairie, we have so few sounds—windmills churning, cows murmuring, the occasional '85 Ford Econoline backfiring on a dusty county road.

Sometimes we need our words to sing.

Sometimes we need silence.

That summer I interned for *South Dakota Magazine*, working for Bernie Hunhoff, our wavy-haired editor who wore denim on denim and wanted me to write about the nostalgia of the place. So I started in about the resurgence of the pallid sturgeon in the Missouri River.

"That fish has been down there since the dinosaur times," the state's biologist told me.

Then, I wrote about two rodeo champions living out in tiny Oelrichs (population 117), on the state's western edge.

"Is it surprising?" I asked the champion barrel racer. "You know, to become a champion from such a small town?"

I heard her spit tobacco juice into a Mountain Dew bottle.

"Not really," she replied, smitten by my greenhorn interrogatives.

"Tough to own horses in the city, son."

The gig didn't pay much. But the duties ate up hours and gave me needed distraction. One day, Bernie even took me riding on a sailboat atop Lewis and Clark Lake.

"There's a lot of beauty here that people don't see," Bernie said, pointing to the homes up on the bluffs overlooking the Missouri River.

"But there are people who will ruin everything."

I stared up, my Subway sandwich at my mouth, a bottle of grape juice rolling at my feet. Those boxy, white homes with plastic-y black trim loomed like a Nantucket whaling captain's quarters high above the river.

"What's wrong with being near the river, you also have to be on it," Bernie continued.

It was the politics of prepositions, and for a second, I saw the land a little clearer. Grasslands waved over the blue river from us. I imagined the chalk cliffs as the first boat hesitantly plunged upriver.

"Just imagine what it used to be," my boss muttered.

But the past didn't provide me any escape, either. Soon, my own melancholy fused with the state's history. Writing a story on trout fishing in the Black Hills, I saw her—Heather—in the stream in hip waders. Another night, after reading about the wild saloon and brothel days in Deadwood, long-faced and sunken-eyed from no sleep, I brushed my teeth only to imagine her in the golden, lion-footed bathtub, her pink toes on the ceramic and the suds coming up to her chin.

It was some madness I was nursing.

I was stuck in what *used-ta-be*.

On another night, my grandma and I drove down to Spink, a few miles west of Iowa, to a slanted-roof café, where all manner of deep-fat-fried foods could be microwaved, she pointed out all the *used-ta-be* places.

"That's where the Johnsons used to farm. That's where the creamery *used-ta-be*."

Now it was a grassy lot, save a couple houses and an old café.

Everything down there—her homestead, her church, the old dance hall called the Ritz—was *used-ta-be.*

And I needed to escape.

On the day I snapped, I was interviewing an old-timer about Yankton College, long since closed down for a federal prison, for old-timey stories. He told me he'd grown up in Beresford.

"Excuse me, Orville," I said, stopping the recorder. "Like, Beresford, South Dakota?"

Orville nodded his head, his blue-and-green tartan felt hat.

The population in South Dakota is never wide enough you can't be assured your car mechanic in overalls isn't a second cousin.

"My grandma's from Beresford, Orville."

Orville chomped down on his straw.

"Who's your grandmother?" he asked.

"Delores McGill?"

The old man's eyes widened impossibly like he stared at a ghost.

"My boy," Orville smiled whimsically, making a dainty humming noise. "I sang in a choir with your grandfather, Edmund."

He smooshed a bite of scone into his mouth.

"He was a wonderful musician, too."

And I wrenched my wince at mention of that word into a smile. That night, I started walking.

From the highway running adjacent Vermillion River, between a few large cottonwood trees, I spied the whitish strip of chalk cliffs hovering over the distant Missouri. A red-tailed hawk sat atop a stop sign. A tan strip of gravel shouldered a periwinkle highway. A cottonwood shook, the blue river wheeled around sandbars trekked in with occasional footprints, tire tracks, maybe a tossed-off can of Busch Light, and around the bend seeing the road leading to the bridge, I breathed deeply, my lungs quivering with exhaustion, and yelled, "I'M NOT A MUSIC—"

Bzzzzzzzzzzzzz.

A bicycle tire!

Maybe it was Heather! I knew she rode her bike on this stretch of pavement for fitness, and I imagined—what sheer, contrived luck—turning to see her long, tan legs pumping up and down, barreling down the highway, ready to rescue me in this geologic floodplain, my pining eyes ready to meet hers.

But no.

I violently lurched back into the ditch.

"Ahh!" I cried, involuntarily.

His eyes popped out, too.

"Ahh!" he blurted back.

It was the McDonald's fry chef.

Curiously he'd ridden a cruiser-bike way into the country, laboriously pushing on the pedals, his face, sweaty and confused, only to stare up at me, talking to myself.

"Wait!" I cried, humiliated. "I'm just . . ."

I tried to put a hand to my face. I tried fake-talking on an invisible cell phone. But the fry chef only rotated his head to face the road forward, cranking his bike around the bend, escaping the cattails and cornfields and cottonwoods, leaving me atop the continental shelf, the Craton, all alone, to walk back home.

I stabbed my Converse shoes into the dirt. You cannot have an adventure in a place you know so well. The lion-maned sun exploded into a thousand purple waves west along the river, and I kept walking with darkness sinking, back to town.

Sometimes, when people ask how I found the Champagne Music Maker in my life, they think it a ruse. A normal twenty-two year old in 2007? He didn't turn to Lawrence Welk, who had been dead for fifteen years. A young, strapping college graduate with a magazine internship does not seek the path of a posthumous polka hero.

But I was lost. I was in the middle of the country. And I needed guidance, even from the unlikeliest of people. So I often give a truncated version. I tell about the fry chef, but I never explain trudging into town, with the bluffs of Vermillion—a city named for its redness by the Lakota people—standing steady in the distance, my only consolation the music of the wind rushing through the tall grass, birds chirping, and the cicadas *see-see-see-see-saawwing*, like a natural symphony bereft a conductor.

CHAPTER 3

MY GRANDMA'S HOUSE IN BERESFORD, SOUTH DAKOTA

SATURDAY, JUNE 16, 2007

Sometimes on nights when the wind blows right off the Potomac, I can almost feel the prairie, my grandparents dancing on balmy summer nights in the Missouri River Valley. I imagine my grandfather, the singer, grabbing the hand of my grandmother, exposing moon-splashed necks. In the corner, the band, a stout, but virile gaggle of gold horns and pink leis, maybe a few condensing bottles of beer by the music stand, sweat brimming through the starched shirts, wiping brows with yellowing rags, started up with a couple of golden, pure notes, like distilled wheat beer on a summer night. Then the dancers, twenty or more thick, packed close-like, two shoots of the same upward branch, begin dipping and cycling like cogs in a giant bronze clock across the floor, while the band—now a pumping, humming, choo-chooing engine—dynamos the room into the white-hot eyehole of delirium, a never-ending wedding dance cakewalk. After that they probably went out behind the barn, put their wet lips on the glass bottles and stared out without seeing over vast, dark, moonlit fields, a corn crop just starting to reach the height of their heaving breasts.

But I am apart from all of that now. So my homeland only comes in glimpses. Recently, for example, I heard the *vrrrt* of needle touching a spinning record, and soon a fizzy organ and glockenspiel waltzed up from the main floor of our home. A stack of the man's records sat in a crate in the living room.

"No!" I called. "I don't listen to his music."

"What?" Carrie called. "You just like to read about him?"

Five minutes later, I heard, "Good grief, is every song like this?"

The sounds twirled down the dark hallway, toward me at the keyboard, where I had been working to put on paper what sounds surrounded me so many summers ago out on the prairie.

———

On the morning after my botched walk to Nebraska, a hot, Saturday morning in 2007, I drove back up old Highway 71, a purplish road coated in quartzite sprinkles mined along the Big Sioux River, to my grandma's.

A couple of windmills, a loping blue-greyish hound in the ditch, and maybe an ATV all got passed on the road that day.

It was time to move Grandma to the nursing home.

After a half hour or so, I pulled my Cavalier into Beresford, where a dozen cars with license plates from Nebraska to Indiana lined the purple-crusted street outside Grandma's house. In the driveway, I could already see my uncle, Tommy, smoking a cigarette, pacing in a polo tucked into denim jeans, debating with his younger brother, Billy, about the origins of a black cash register Billy was taking out to his car.

All families, in fairness, do this. You take the antique cash register. The furniture. The silverware. All objects—even the quotidian—contain depreciable love.

The family thought it'd be nice for Grandma to see all of her possessions find a new home before moving into the nursing home. And the timing worked for me, too. Needing to furnish my new apartment, I hoped for an ottoman or maybe a decorative Irish tin whistle. But when I walked in, surprising me, Aunt Rosemary thrust into my chest a book: *Wunnerful, Wunnerful: The Autobiography of Lawrence Welk*.

Grinning up at me, waving a baton was the man my father calls the Polka Elvis.

"What do I need this for?" I asked.

"Just take it," said Rosemary. "Otherwise, we'll dump it at the library."

By this Saturday morning in 2007, I knew the man, of course. On my dad's side, family legend revolved around Welk being some cheapskate. On my mom's side, the maestro apparently befriended my grandfather's cousin, Edna Stoner, writing to her regularly from the road. But I wanted a swashbuckling romance by a forgotten prairie novelist or maybe an old diary of Grandma's eldest sister, Aggie, who'd been the county beauty and swept off her feet by a cowboy from Gann Valley, only to die at twenty-five of tuberculosis. Anyway, I didn't want something rotting in a Wal-Mart bargain bin.

"You never know what kind of stories you might find in there," said Aunt Rosemary, who moonlighted herself on the piano at a country club in Des Moines. "He was quite a musician."

There was that word again. That cocklebur stuck to my sleeve.

When I looked down, again, maybe the angle of the light through the recently Windex-shined kitchen windows came stronger, this geriatric band leader with a baton, slicked-back hair, and maroon suit with striped tie was looking back.

I know this sounds crazy, but his green eyes seemed to follow me. No amount of Santa Monica airbrushing could cover up those eyes. They were smiling, with the tiniest crow's feet. Between snaps of a flash bulb, the photographer captured the smallest pain. Welk looked tired, like someone who learned long ago to smile for a living.

Welk looked like a musician.

Flipping open the first few pages, standing on the linoleum floor of my grandmother's kitchen, a glittering image suddenly played like an old projector of a touring automobile hurtling on a Saturday down a dusty Dakota road with a gaggle of brass instruments sticking out the back, golden necks and bells bobbing over circulating, rubber tires.

I turned another page, and some Dust Bowl big band called the Honolulu Fruit Gum Orchestra stared back at me. Flipping forward a few pages, I saw a bunch of familiar town names: Aberdeen, Sioux City, Yankton. And that earth came rushing forward.

Finally, leaning against the green, rotary telephone, the cord drooping next to emergency numbers, I'd stopped on a glossy photograph in the middle of the book.

"Is this her?" I asked, holding up the photograph.

An old woman with mouth ajar sat in a bed, improbably, below a stage surrounded by Welk and His Champagne Music Makers. I inspected the cutline: "Edna Stoner, at the World's Only Corn Palace in Mitchell, South Dakota."

"Bless us and save us!" said Aunt Pat, laughing. "There's old Aunt Edna."

For one more time, the kitchen filled with conversation.

But then my mother, tall and black-haired, like me, appeared. Her blue eyes narrowed on me.

"You don't want that book," she scolded.

Then she walked over and snatched the book from my hand.

"This isn't yours," she said, waving the book like an impassioned parish priest.

"Hey!" I cried. "I was going to read that!"

My mother flipped open the inside jacket, revealing Lawrence Welk's signature, written in black Sharpie marker.

"But it's an autographed copy, Christopher," said Mom, looking to Rosemary. "Don't you want it back?"

My aunt, recoiling from this melodrama, shook her head, "No way."

Spurned, my mom turned to her own mother, sitting at the wooden table, sipping lemonade coolly.

"How 'bout it, Mom? You'll want something to read in the home, right?"

But my grandmother, graciously, almost with a knowledge of this bequeathing, just laughed like a clarinet.

"Why would I want to read that?"

Then, tired of this falderal, Rosemary—the eldest sibling—walked over and took the book from her youngest sister and placed it into her nephew's hands.

And she gave me a look I'll never forget, wary and concerned, like someone deciding whether to choose right or left at an unmarked fork in the road in the middle of the night.

"Make sure you read it, at least."

So I slapped a slab of painter's tape over Welk's face, wrote "Christopher" in blue ink pen, and carried the prize out to my car.

When I came back in, everyone had left the kitchen, with Rosemary tying a green bandana around her black hair, smoking a cigarette, mumbling to herself, "Why would I want that book? None of the good stories are in there anyway."

I had inherited my escape.

The cicadas buzzed *see-see-see-saaaw*. It was a Saturday night. No gig. No girlfriend. And when I drove back down to Vermillion, my tires crunching over the pink gravel, the windows open, I drove almost parallel with those ATVs caterwauling through the grassy ditch.

CHAPTER 4

ON THE BIG PORCH AT 123 FOREST AVENUE IN VERMILLION, SOUTH DAKOTA

SATURDAY, JUNE 16, 2007

One evening, back when we lived in Sioux Falls, Carrie came home from work with a surprise.

"My coworker's mother went on a date with Lawrence Welk."

She set down her brown purse on the kitchen island table.

"And guess why there weren't any more dates?"

Her round face glowed bright red behind her black, framed glasses.

I was still too shocked to speak.

"Lawrence was 'too handsy.'"

Like other keystone species out on the Great Plains—the rambunctious, squeaky prairie dog or the bluestem prairie grass, with its leviathan root system below the earth—Lawrence Welk is going extinct.

In early 2021, I called down to the offices at South Dakota Public Broadcasting.

"Hey," I asked. "So who does get the highest rating each week? Out of the shows, I mean."

The man didn't take any time to shoot back that answer, as if he'd had it written out on a legal pad, waiting for someone to call up with just that inquiry.

"Why, Lawrence Welk," came the response, short and punchy. "He gets about a 10 percent market share each week at his time slot. That's about a 9 percent increase from what we usually get."

"Figures," I said.

"But," the man shot back, in a bit of bombast I've had a difficult time forgiving. "You got to remember, that Welk's audience is almost entirely sixty-five and plus. It's on in all the nursing homes!"

Even in North Dakota, they're increasingly skeptical the television accordionist is worth perpetually celebrating, now going on three decades removed from his death. A couple years back, their biennial, bicameral legislative organ up there in Bismarck found its way into a scrum when considering buying up the Welk Family Estate outside Strasburg.

"What," the secretary of the treasury pointedly asked at one juncture, "are we going to buy up Phil Jackson's dorm room next?"

Eventually someone pointed out that the great state of North Dakota failed to count amongst its fleet of properties an honest-to-goodness sod house, and that's how Old Man Ludwig Welk's homestead was bought right up.

But there are still places of the Upper Midwest where Welk echoes across a shelter belt, trapped in a tin bait bucket out by the Jim River.

Carrie's coworker, Cassie, baked us a meatloaf on a cold Monday evening for our dinner, and then we moved to the sofa, where I took out my phone to record the conversation, setting it down atop the plush champagne carpet.

"So where to begin?" asked Doris, Cassie's mother and Welk's romantic liaison's daughter. "First off, I'm not sure what you've been told."

"Oh?" I asked.

"Mom said she wouldn't date him because he couldn't speak the English language."

Cassie, sitting next to her husband, a contemplative truck driver, harumphed. Then she offered a plate of cheese and crackers.

"Maybe that's what a mother tells a daughter versus what a mother tells a granddaughter."

I returned to Vermillion that Saturday evening in 2007 to what my landlord called a "sleeping suite," which was a room atop a gargantuan Victorian house, which shorted out regularly if the microwave and television were running at the same time. Thankfully, I got to use the porch. And to the porch I descended, stretching out, the chains tensing, and pulling out the book with a turquoise green dust jacket, fingering the stiff, white pages, suntanned along the foxed edge.

Next door, a professor played with his children and their Golden Retriever on a slip-n-slide. Across the street, a teenager read on a wide porch. So with the summer lazily rolling up its sleeves, loosening its tie, I feathered the pages of *Wunnerful, Wunnerful.*

Curiously, the frayed binding cracked ever so lightly. A puff of stale bubblegum odor wafted into my nostrils.

"Whoa!"

The pages of this tome had been squeezed for maybe thirty years. Sundogs of the faintest caramel tiptoed along the margins. The paper felt crisp to the touch. It was a book all right. Nice and weighty in my hands.

And then I read the very first sentence Lawrence Welk wrote: "When I was about three years old, my mother used to say in her soft voice to one of my sisters, 'Would you please go outside and find Lawrence for me?'"

"'And if we couldn't find you in the yard,' says my sister Barbara, 'then we'd always go and look in the summer kitchen—and there you'd be, trying to make a violin.'"

I suppressed a giggle, like one stifles a geyser of soda pop bubbling up your nose.

The text was so formal, delicate.

Curious, I plunged forward. On the bluffs, heavy trees, wooden spandrels glowing from the sunset across the street, I strangely felt pulled onward into a glowing, sentient past, page by crisp white page.

The tale of the sixth child of Christine and Ludwig Welk is a song.

Lawrence was born in 1903 to immigrants from Odessa, ethnic Alsatians who had lugged a Bible, an accordion, and two perplexed oxen one hundred miles from the railhead in Ipswich, South Dakota, to Strasburg, North Dakota.[1] His childhood was not pleasant. In that remote parcel of North Dakota, Lawrence slouched to milk cows, proved inefficient at working the bellows in the blacksmith shop with his father, and earned the nickname "the Dumer-Esel" from his family.[2]

Most importantly for his long-shot musical ambitions, however, at least according to his book, when he was still a boy, Lawrence nearly died.

As early as page three or thereabouts, at the age of eleven, Lawrence wakes one night with a feeble cough echoing off the wood frame inside the sod-insulated home.

"Lawrencell!" yelled his father, lovingly. "You keep it down!"[3]

Achoo-achoo-achoo in the night air like the mourning dove.

"Ludwig," his wife, Christine said, rolling over. "Get up. That cough is not natural."

"No, the boy will be fine . . . Lawrence!" he hollered again.

Lawrence wearily repeats his rosary, trying to coax sleep, under

---

1. His ancestors had been lulled into trying their game in Ukraine by Czar Catherine the Great, an ethnic German, before post-Prussian Wars disfavor sent them scrambling.
2. Which I believe is German for "the Little Jackass."
3. This isn't actually what was said in the text of that little book, but if you want that, read it yourself.

dizzying pain. At the breakfast table the next day, his siblings chatted about the morning, but the boy stared woefully at his oatmeal.

"No time like the present," his brother Louie said.

They slid chairs under the table. The sisters—Ann Mary, Barbara—followed the brothers, Louie, Mike, and Lawrence. They walked toward the barn over tawny, shorn grass, the sun tilting up, when their slightest brother fell dead to the ground.

"Lawrence! Lawrence!"

Ludwig was in the shop, pounding a hammer upon a red-hot horseshoe. But cries such as these always reach mothers first. Like the wind, Christine flew across the grass, her white cotton hem curling against the ground.

"Son! Please get up. Son!"

According to *Wunnerful, Wunnerful,* the family lifted Lawrence into a cousin's car and rode seventy miles to Bismarck.[4] For two weeks, they kneeled at his bedside while the nuns of mercy inserted needles and tubes into the boy and sipped him medicine from a spoon. Eventually, Lawrence would awake and remember nothing.

Except for his dream.

The angel-headed farm boy saw himself as a hawk, or some winged creature, the sun luring him to whirling upward, spiraling higher, and at each progressive altitude out over the square fields and ranch-style houses with a satellite in back and a pickup out front,[5] Lawrence felt more and more wonderful, he says, relieved of his pain, seeing the land beneath that stretched for miles and miles. When he woke, two nurses were pulling him from the walls of the hospital room, his fingers falcate and sweaty.

According to his memoir, Lawrence would convalesce at home, near the mahogany pump organ, its rolling wood, the dark pedals, the soft, white keys. After two months, miraculously, he sat up in bed. After three, he played on his father's accordion. Sweetness wheezing slowly wraps around his bony shoulders, as Lawrence's small fingers ambled like ducks following a mother up the white keys, the

---

4. And the adroit—if, at time bombastic—prose of Bernice McGeehan, the book's coauthor.
5. That's actually not accurate, but let's go with it.

heavy wooden instrument garnished in bronze plates slugged into his caved chest.

The polkas, the mazurkas, the schottisches.

"Now a thought so exciting," writes Lawrence, with the aid of that amanuensis Bernice McGeehan,[6] "so overpowering that I could scarcely bear to think of it, began to inch its way forward into my mind. Maybe I wouldn't have to be a farmer! Maybe, just maybe, I could earn a living as a musician!"

When his mother, Christine, brings dishes of dumplings and soups to the table at night, Lawrence skips over from the barn, his skin still stretched tightly over his chest bones, a small extra flap of skin visible under his Adam's apple where the tube had been inserted, the boy would listen contentedly as his father and brothers talked about their days at school or in fields. His soft green eyes bolted from sibling to sibling.

"Read Goethe."

"Learned about a solar system."

In the summer, "Cut grass."

"Drove plough."

In the fall, "Shot jackrabbits."

"Shoveled manure" in the spring.

None of it envied Lawrence.

When questioned on his day, he'd meekly report.

"I made music."

It's what he wanted to answer everyday thereafter.

"What did you do today, Lawrencell?"

"I-I-I made music."

Within an hour out there on the porch swing of 123 Forest Avenue, gnats circling overhead, my shoulders rigid against the bench, I'd read his whole, blasted childhood. Street lamps glowed. I was unsure if anyone within the last fifteen, twenty, shoot, even thirty years

---

6. As I've alluded to, a real gravedigger of a prose artist.

had touched this text. But it still held up, like an old Ford Econoline out in the garage just needs air in the tires and an oil change.

By nightfall, with the children going inside, the water sprinkler gurgling to a stop, I could recite a new coterie of facts and figures about this unlikely prairie Mozart floating in my mind like music to those wheat field symphonies.

Q: Where did Lawrence get his first accordion?

A: From his father. It cost like $700, which is the price of a Jaguar by today's standards. Lawrence agreed to indentured servitude of four years—until his twenty-first birthday—if his father coughed up the cash for a handmade European model. When it arrived, Lawrence spent the night harassing his family and the livestock with schottisches.

Q: Where did Lawrence learn English?

A: From those Ursuline nuns. Lawrence grew up on a sheet of wheat the length of the eastern seaboard. That German accent—while initially problematic in his parents' new country—helped out in the long run, as nothing said "authentic polka man" to millions of Americans at home watching television during the 1950s, '60s, and '70s as someone who slurred the phrase, "Penn-sil-vain-ya Pol-ka" with rapidity.

Q: Was Welk the best in the family on the accordion?

A: Debatable. He once toured the Upper Midwest as "North America's Foremost Accordionist," but after a three-day wedding, one neighbor drunk on peach schnapps told him, "You're pretty good on the accordion there Lawrence. But you're not as good as your father. You just don't have the rhythm." More Freudian fire—in my estimation—for his simmering feud with Ludwig.

The book, as I've intimated, was a hagiography—like that night Welk endured a livid parish priest in Ipswich, South Dakota, railing against him, some devil, for playing a fundraiser past midnight and leading the depraved parishioners "dancing and prancing onto the Sabbath." And, of course, there was his capitalistic advancements, speaking of walking along the boardwalk at an Iowa theme park and hearing all the best bands duke it out for dancers, some Adam Smith type calculation.

But there was one passage in his book that hooked me the most.

On the porch, I read about Lawrence's relationships: a wholesome tryst with a Texan who wouldn't date a papist; a brief courtship of a posh Dane he used to walk up and down the boardwalk with in Arnold's Park, Iowa; and finally the brown-eyed girl sitting among the nursing students at his broadcasts for WNAX Radio in Yankton, South Dakota, who looked "unimpressed by everything that was going on around her."

"Oh that's Fern Renner," a friend is quoted as saying, "You won't get anyplace with her. She's not only a nurse—she wants to be a doctor."

But Lawrence pursued the reluctant Fern. She, naturally, avoided him. He played opportunistically by opting for elective surgery at her hospital to remove that pesky skin flap on his neck, so she was forced to care for him. He almost died from blood loss during surgery. The formerly adverse Fern felt guilty and went on a date with him. She then moved to Texas, seemingly putting a stopper on that little season of life, but eventually, perhaps homesick, she relented to his hounding and married him.

It was what he wrote, though, that propelled me nearly off the porch-swing: "There was a whole group of girls known as 'band girls' who used to hang around the bandstand in every town we played, and they were as different from Fern as night from day."

And I stood up.

Looking vacantly out from that porch hanging off a Victorian house into the tawny streetlight of downtown Vermillion, I heard her name. Heather, I thought painfully.

That was the same with me and Heather.

Bemused, I looked back down to the book, to that person with the bulbous nose and maroon leisure suit and asinine green tie.

I couldn't read more tonight.

Streetlamps glowed orange along the darkened Forest Avenue, the professor's children long ago going inside, even the gardening neighbor to the north, with her big floppy hat, escaped from the mosquitos. Crumpled Capri Suns lay at my feet.

Balancing myself, the wood under my feet creaking, I tucked the book under my elbow, swatted at the incredulously large beach ball of mosquitos dangling below the amber porch light, and I traipsed back upstairs in a hypnotic daze, collapsing into a deep, catatonic sleep.

CHAPTER 5

THE PHOENIX LOUNGE IN HARRISBURG, SOUTH DAKOTA

THURSDAY, JUNE 23, 2007

My college band, the Brickhouse Boys, played what was supposed to be our last gig of summer at the Phoenix Lounge in Harrisburg, a quiet suburb south of Sioux Falls, on the Saturday before Memorial Day.

Let me clarify: the Phoenix Lounge was not some swanky, Vegas-style cabaret. There would be no spiritual rebirths either, save for those perhaps experienced by the guys who drank enough watery grain beer to fall off their stools before night's end.

But I'd gotten used to this. That was one of the first rules of the prairie rock scene of the early 2000s: the name of something was never the actual something. During the band's brief tenure, we played the Safari Lounge in Brookings, which had nothing to do with big game, just drunk farmhouse boys from Ipswich; a bar dubiously called World Imports in downtown Sioux Falls that earned its cosmopolitan reputation for serving Heineken; and the Phoenix Lounge, which, as I've intimated, was really just a slouching tavern adjacent to a cornfield. Frankly, the only accurately named place we stopped on tour would be 7th St Entry, which was, as advertised, a doorway to a club on 7th Street in downtown Minneapolis.

Still, I had hopes. What has always troubled me about music on the prairie is the language. I often want it to be sharper, less fuzzy, more exact. That night, just days after Heather and I broke up, I had latched onto whimsical delusions when Donny told me, "We're playing the *Phoenix Lounge*, Chris. Be there at 8."

But as I rolled in with my keyboard, named "Kurt" for my favorite author (Vonnegut), its case plastered by a fraying "Tom Vilsack for President" sticker, I navigated between some old-timers in seed caps at the bar and felt neither the promise of rebirth nor sophisticated leisure.

"Honey, you look like Rob Thomas," observed the bartender, her black bra visible beneath a sheer blouse. "You better be as smooth on those ivories as you are on the eyes."

And I prepared for what was to be the longest night of my life.

From the get-go, the mood was off. The sound guys used the speakers and mixers salvaged before Sioux Falls paved over the Pomp Room, the same stacks Aerosmith and Janitor Bob and the Armchair Cowboys played into. But that was lost on me and my brother.

A guy with grey, scraggly hair collapsed under his red beret yelled to Leo, who stood at the microphone, "Sing into that mic like the most beautiful woman in the world just walked in and grabbed your crotch!" Leo just self-consciously blushed.

Then the opening band—this all-instrumental, jam band trio called Governor's Suite—got into a small fight with our lead singer. Let me preface: Governor's Suite was good, no doubt. Tight, technical rhythms and all that. But they were super boring. And jam bands were sort of passé by 2007. The iPod generation had grown weary of standing in fields for twenty-five-minute songs with sax solos.

So after their lead guitarist thanked the dozen people, Bobby Vice ran up on stage. "Don't leave yet!" he exclaimed to the crowd. "We're not, you know," and then he pointed at Governor's Suite. "*That.*"

I just figured they'd take the comment in stride, because I figured everyone in the scene knew Bobby was laying the pipes for a future *Rolling Stone* profile, where a middle-aged journalist would descend on rural Harrisburg and interview the chain-smoking band director to find out, yeah, twenty years ago when he—fronting a mathematically proficient albeit stupefyingly dry jam band—opened up for the one-and-only Bobby Vice. Bobby knew even then he was too big, too good for this backwater hayseed territory.

But Governor's Suite didn't see it that way. They said some words, then left with all their hemp-skirted fans in their painted van, abandoning us with virtually nobody in the audience. Even the sound guys joined the Dekalb caps at the bar. Worse, we had to cover four hours. And with only one hour of original music, we'd need to rely on our addendum of covers, which ranged from the Clash to Amy Winehouse.

But a miracle occurred: Bobby strutted around stage between songs; Monster danced with the bartender; Poncho played extended guitar solos; Donny took frequent smoke breaks; and I satisfied Gershwin-ian longings by jangling my piano like a chandelier drop. Somehow, midnight arrived. Bar-close was in sight. After a slurp of Grain Belt, we started up the originals again, and by 1 a.m., we could see light, revving up our covers and eventually landing on Randy Newman's "Short People."

"Short People" is a quirky song. Satirical, sure. Even politically incorrect. The tune had been banned across the nation except for in the Sioux Empire, where sensitivity to Newman's yoking of "short people" must have struck people as an affront against political correctness.[1] Nevertheless, I blanched at playing the tune again, for the third time, but Donny clicked his sticks, yelling, "Who's gonna know? Let's just get out of here."

So we started in. Almost immediately, two sets of headlights from pickups pivoted off the highway, parked outside the bar, and then the drivers—and their dates—swung the Phoenix's door open. In walked two middle-aged couples, hands raised like it was Mardis Gras.

"Stupid people!" cried one man, who rushed the empty, diamond-checkered dance floor. "I love that song! 'Stupid people' got no one to love!'"

---

1. Albeit as an extended analogy for the silliness of prejudice.

"Keep playing, boys!" yelled his wife, gyrating in tall, leather hunting boots. "We came to dance!"

It's not an exaggeration to say this was the night I almost lost music. Partly because of my thoughts on Heather. I kept thinking about her, cuddled up on her couch under a blanket, reading in the cottage she rented from her dad. I wanted that. But, more than just Heather, I wanted that normalness. For most of college, I'd been a pretty boring kid. I lived in a Catholic Church, for cripes' sake. But then my band came along and *whammo*. I was now playing Randy Newman covers to an empty bar in a cornfield.

I didn't know how to get out of this. Even if my future didn't involve Heather and that couch, what would it be? And how could I get back on the right road?

The band wanted to be done. We'd spurned their longneck-beer-bottle entreaties. Bobby even falsely told them, "Copyright law prevents us from playing the same Randy Newman song thrice in one night."

But the bartender got involved. Like a cigarette-lunged God speaking to Moses, a voice from the PA system filled the bar. "You boys got another Randy Newman in ya?"

We hadn't heard from her all night. Now she apparently favored our satirical selection. But she also had about $200 in that Corona tin at the bar for us.

So Donny rattled his snare drum. "'Short People,' man. It's what they want." And a South Dakota band knows it's half-vodka, half-Red Bull. You can't be a purist.

"We're just a jukebox they placed a quarter into," said Donny.

So we reared back for another.

That night, in what would be an otherwise forgotten night in the history of music, my band played Randy Newman's "Short People" three, possibly four times in a row to four rowdy fans (five, counting the bartender) to stave off getting skunked by the venue. The verses, choruses, and bridge just merged. But we had an ordained purpose. We stretched our musical loaves and fishes all the way to closing time, somewhere around 1:50 a.m., maybe even fully 2 a.m., as our audience rode each other's thighs, cocking back their heads and yelling out "Stupid People!" every time the chorus hit.

By night's end, the gear all packed away, Bobby and I pulled $200 in sweaty dollars from the bottom of that Corona tin.

"Did okay for yourself, Rob Thomas," said the bartender, with a wink.

Sometime around 3 a.m., standing underneath a gas station island as a halo of bugs hovered over my head as I pumped gas, my brother stared off into the darkness of the countryside, a single barn light twinkling off in the distance.

"Hey, where was Heather tonight?" he asked.

I had forgotten I hadn't told him. Hanging up the nozzle, I checked the price on the screen, hoping my credit card would clear in the morning.

"She won't be coming around much anymore," is all I said.

And Leo looked at me, nodding, sensing my pain like a brother does. We didn't talk about this stuff in my family much. We didn't have the language for it. But we had ways to communicate hurt just the same. You don't need words for that. Sometimes music can do. Sometimes silence. We drove back home, reaching our parents' house in Minnesota just as the morning sun peeked over the abandoned train east of town.

After that night, as far as I understood, I blamed music. Music couldn't be trusted. Back in Vermillion, up there in my sleeping suite, my piano sat under a pile of clothes and a rotating fan. I had no intention of clearing it off, even after that second night of reading Welk's mellifluous story. When I came upstairs, I spotted my piano, Kurt, and briefly felt a tug to hear it sing before I kicked that idea out of mind.

Monday morning, I drove to the offices of *South Dakota Magazine* and sat in the cushy chair. The electrons in my brain—dazzling for days after starting *Wunnerful, Wunnerful*—settled again into a machinelike hum. The ragamuffin dog laid her head on my feet. My tired eyes scanned archived magazines for historical curios to complete a "This Day in History" calendar for the website.

Everything again felt like historical reenactment. People canoed the Missouri River using Lewis and Clark's route. Wagon-wheelers errantly traced the settlers' path. An actor still shot Wild Bill Hickok at 4 p.m. every single day out on the streets of Deadwood.

For lunch, I ate a bologna sandwich in the parking lot near the baseball diamond along the river. Trucks moseyed in. Trucks moseyed out. I sipped my Coca-Cola, wondering what movie the Coyote Twin was showing that night, when I got a text message from Bobby Vice, our singer.

Bobby Vice, for what it's worth, was two years younger than me. Each Midwestern state college student body is allotted at least one campus rock star. Maybe two. He was all snakeskin boots, wild, black hair, and tight denim jeans. We first started the band in the offices of the *Volante*, USD's student newspaper. After hand-pressing melodies and songs together at the old mahogany piano in the St. Thomas More Newman Center sanctuary, we had T-shirt ideas, but not a name.

"What do you think about the Bookhouse Boys?" Bobby had asked above the clinks of Red Stripe and squeaking, dissonant saxophone one jazz night at Open Mic's Bar.

I told Bobby I dug co-opting a fairytale name.

"Three little pigs, right?!"

"No, *book*house," he said. "From *Twin Peaks?*"

My cultural oeuvre had yet to extend to David Lynch and that early 1990s cult television show.

Our first drummer, Egan, however, knew that, like saying *Rumplestiltsken*, the name stuck.

"Brickhouse is a cool name," he sternly warned. "Can't change it now."

With the language aligned, the band suddenly existed. But bands could disappear, too. You only needed one member to start the unraveling process, and the words could scatter into the wind.

I didn't expect to hear from Bobby after the Phoenix Lounge show. I didn't think any of this would be happening, mostly because Bobby's band and Donny's band were both supposed to be going on all-summer tours.

But that all changed.

"Steve found God," Bobby told me over the phone, while I sat in the parking lot near the Yankton baseball field.

"What?" I asked.

"Yeah, I didn't see that coming, either," Bobby said. "I thought Steve was a godless punk."

Steve was the Throwback's drummer. The Throwback, a kind of Dave Grohl-via-Iggy-Pop ensemble, was Bobby's main band.

"We moved Donny to drums and got Tom on bass."

But Bobby explained Tom was a thirty-five-year-old father of three and bald.

"So that doesn't work, either. I gave him a baseball cap," Bobby continued, "for tour, you know, but turns out he can't take work off."

"Oh?"

"And I've got to get out of Vermillion this summer. I've got to go on tour."

Sometimes when one band died, like saplings sprouting up in the aftermath of a large cottonwood flattened by wind, another band emerged into the sunlight.

"So what do you say? You want to go on tour?"

On my rainy ride home to Vermillion that night, a thought flickered like the wings of a grasshopper lodged in a cheap car's grill: maybe I am a musician.

For the first time in a month, I tossed the clothing off my Kurz-weil and played songs no one yet knew, my book tossed on the cheap futon, thinking about all the music we could've played to that crowd the night at the Phoenix to make them really fly.

CHAPTER 6

THE OAHE BALLROOM IN PIERRE, SOUTH DAKOTA

MONDAY, JULY 23, 2007

There were a lot of good reasons for a band like ours to stay home.

First off, it was a rule that no self-respecting band opens a tour on a Monday. Bands don't play Mondays. They're the sabbath.

Second off, we were playing Pierre (pronounced like the boat dock, not the French word), the capitol of South Dakota. That was another rule. Bands are supposed to see the world on tour. Pierre was not the world. It was about three hours from anything, situated below mild, bald bluffs at the confluence of the Missouri and Bad Rivers.

After Pierre brought us to the third rule we broke: we didn't have any more shows lined up. You need shows for a tour. We had roughly two weeks set aside for tour, with each night reading "TBA," according to our MySpace page.

Nevertheless, on the second to last Monday in July, we boarded into our crudely-named van that for our purposes here I will just refer to as the SS *Robert Bly*, and drove west down Interstate 90 toward Pierre.

With the windows down, Bobby searched for tunes on KOYA coming out of Rosebud while my lanky brother chatted with Poncho about Prince's rotating backing band. Donny paddled the knuckles of his thumbs on the steering column, and there in back, squeezing a pillow, Monster stretched his legs out on the floor-to-ceiling steel fence separating the more precious cargo (us) from the rattling amps, guitars, and keyboards that shook and flew forward at every impromptu stop.

But, pleased to be escaping Vermillion, I just stared out the window, the countryside passing by flat as ever, and billboards like poetry flew in the air.

JOE'S TOW TRUCK SERVICE.
WE <u>REJECT</u> ANIMAL RIGHTS' ACTIVISTS.
<u>REAL</u> PROPS FROM DANCES WITH WOLVES.

Eastern South Dakota is so flat they post billboards to keep people's minds from going crazy. You read 'em. You get distracted. Eventually unamused by those, I unzipped my duffel bag. My hand rummaged for a laptop and struck my book instead.

Over the last month, I had finished the Welk book. But I wanted to read it again, to find out how Lawrence—just this regular guy doing what regulars loved, even if sophisticated culture was left staring in confusion at him—could pioneer a trail for us.

So I opened to the dogear, leaned back as the sun and wind eked through the vinyl window, and I fell back into the music of yesteryear.

Eighty-seven years earlier, and approximately 108 miles north from us, Lawrence was blowing his first big break at the Assumption Day Festival at St. Peter and Paul's Catholic Church in Hague, North Dakota (population 315).

The aspirational bandleader from hay country had littered the tri-county with hand-painted German advertisements, practiced his accordion, and rented out something called the "Opera Hall."

But when he arrived at the hall (after mass) to sell tickets, there wasn't a soul in line.

Nobody would be coming!

And at a three-dollar rental cost with gas money also gone, Lawrence needed to fill the hall in order to break even—no sure thing with those picky polka connoisseurs. So, terrified of speaking to strangers, he breathed deeply and summoned up all his courage. To save that night's engagement, he would need to promote the hell out of it.

That night, when we pulled up to the dubiously named Oahe Ballroom (a conference room in a roadside motel), two vans were parked, and a few Native boys rolled around on skates.

"Over here!" called Taman.

Inside the venue, a rat-haired DJ and guitarist pounded away, while a dozen or so alt-teens swirled in the mosh pit. I deflated a little bit. This wasn't exactly like Lawrence Welk's gigs. But I knew we wouldn't hit paydirt immediately.

So while the opening band rumbled on, I finished carrying in my gear and then skipped outside, where I found a white plastic chair near a 7 Up machine and kicked up my legs to watch the sunset over the bluffs, remembering what I learned from the little, red book.

Tickets were a dollar, so Lawrence hit up the Germans first. He carried a spool of ribbon and for one dollar used his scissors to snip off a strip that dancers pinned to their shirtsleeves. Ladies, of course, were free, but he bartered with a group of five bachelor farmers.

"Then how about the five of you for two-and-a-half?"

"Sold!"

Around 6 p.m., Lawrence downed a coffee and hamburger. Next, with the sun still high, he taught those farmers how to dance. They lacked coordination but soon managed something like a two-step, ambling like newborn calves one boot ahead the other. Finally, upon arrival of the ladies, who in their summer dresses ghostwriter Bernice McGeehan (a real utility infielder of a prose artist) says looked like "beautiful prairie flowers," a dark blue descended over the horizon, and after all the ticket purchasers arrived and with no more room in the Hague "Opera House" for latecomers, Lawrence climbed a chair in the corner of the room, briefly admired his own hard day's work, and began the easiest part of any musician's job: the set.

The Brickhouse Boys had played warm-up gigs, including a raucous night at a birthday party at the Wessington Springs Opera House and a food festival on a melted-snow-cone blacktop in Aberdeen. But the band didn't click. Even since the Phoenix, we'd lost a step. Leo nearly fell off stage. Monster accidentally tossed his tambourine into the crowd. Poncho—when he finally found the right chord—soloed over my piano solo. Donny splashed when he should've stung. And Bobby heroically stage-dove.

"Horse whips and chains!" he sang, heading into our hit song, "Rope-a-Dope."

Maybe a dozen, maybe fewer malcontent teenagers raised fists and thrummed their bodies to the beat.

In back, Taman counted our measly cash pile.

"I got thirty dollars for you dudes," he said, with a shoulder shrug.

We were lucky to get that.

Welk's show, by comparison, was an explosion. Dancers spun in fast waltzes, and word soon spread across hay country about this kid having such a banner night that half the town tried getting in.

When he returned to his father's kitchen table in Strasburg, under a kerosene lamp, he set down a pile of money totaling nearly $150.

Ludwig sat with his son at the wooden table, unimpressed.

"Yes. Tonight was good," he said. "But you only make that much every now and then."

Lawrence said he'd expand to bigger cities, Bismarck, maybe Aberdeen!

"A traveling musician, no, that's not the life for you, Lawrence. It's not a good life. You'd run into all kinds of conditions you know nothing about . . . I don't want you to lose your faith and fall into a life of sin."

It's a battle his father was losing. Lawrence, devoutly Catholic, said nothing. He nodded and climbed the ladder outside the home to fall asleep in the same bed he had slept in since childhood, his feet hanging off the end and millions of stars blinking at him through the window.

Wiping sweat off my face, I walked through a hole in the fence and down to the train tracks.

A distant pickup growled.

A lawyer's door shuttered.

The neon cactus over a bar illuminated.

"Hey."

I looked back up to the parking lot.

A young woman in a pencil skirt with black hair, save a single green stripe, stared at me. Her eyes were different colors.

"You guys were genius tonight."

The compliment landed at my feet.

"Really?" I asked, confused. "We were actually really bad."

"Sure, but you've got potential," she said, approaching. Her husky voice didn't match her cleaned-up look. "I can tell you got talent, though. I mean, that piano? Sounds kind of like Radiohead. Name's Josie," she said.

"Christopher," I responded. "I think we actually just played in the old swimming pool room."

"Yeah, you did. But you gotta start somewhere. Also, you got to teach Monster the notes," she continued, coughing, with her tutorial. "And tell your brother to lighten up."

"It's a problem," I said. "With his beekeeper's hat, he can't see much."

"I know, right?" She unbuttoned the pearl snap on her blouse's breast pocket and pulled out a carton of American Spirits. "Anyway, I'm in town for my dad's retirement, and I came down to see my little brother's band. They're the headliners."

"I hear Anorexic Fat Kid is good."

"They're not. But whatever. No one is when they start."

The rapid *thump thump thump* of a bass drum checking levels pounded out the open door.

"But if you ever get to Minneapolis, look me up, hey?"

Before I could ask a follow-up question she had sped into the open doorway, tossing off her cigarette.

From the back of the old swimming pool room, I watched Anorexic Fat Kid implode on stage. They whacked electric guitars and yelped about all the girls in high school who wouldn't look at them. And the stranger with green hair swung her arms out, windmilling over the concrete. She would later tell me that she had wanted to go to art school, but her father—who ran a chain of pharmacies—wouldn't abide. So she went to law school and hated it. She said she worried she would soon wind up in some Sioux Falls cul-de-sac sipping Kahlua, laughing about how "wild and artsy" she used to be.

That was another rule: we were all going to grow out of this.

⸻

With Pierre's neon-bar scene just getting lit, Donny slammed on the gas pedal, and we bulldozed through the intersection. The highway led us straight home.

Cattle in the field. Stars in the sky.

Poncho talked to Leo about musical trivia. Bobby searched the dial for old-school country again. And I stared at the red, blinking dots of distant windmills.

"Don Henley was the drummer?" Leo asked.

"Seriously," replied Poncho. "The sickest."

I tried reading my book but could only make out scribbles on the pages in the lightless van, so I just set it aside, looked out the window, and watched like a child as the miles and miles of dark, indistinguishable, prairie hills rolled like waves on an ancient, black sea, and the moon dangled and twirled like a far-off jewel-encrusted disco ball.

CHAPTER 7

THE WORLD'S ONLY CORN PALACE IN MITCHELL, SOUTH DAKOTA

TUESDAY, JULY 24, 2007 (AROUND 12:03 A.M.)

Two hours later, Donny eased on the gas near Mitchell. The gas station was lit up like a theme park. The guys shuffled in. I walked to the edge of the canopy's light periphery, massaging a kink in my neck from sleeping against the window, and I looked toward downtown, where I knew, somewhere, that glorious castle rose.

The World's Only Corn Palace.

That summer, I had read about the Corn Palace for *South Dakota Magazine*. It's true that the advertising campaign for the Corn Palace opted for billboards with the mind-boggling slogan, "The World's Only Corn Palace."

One might be tempted to ask, is this "only" a necessary distinction? Do you need to, say, emphasize that you're the world's "only" wax fruit museum? Or the "only" electronic jug band?

But I like to think that the researchers at the crack advertising firm hired by the Corn Palace had done their due diligence because, amazingly, in the early 1900s, there had been dozens of palaces across a swath of the region. Numbers fluctuate, but there were possibly thirteen corn palaces in Sioux City alone. A new one every year was built. Sioux City's palatial infrastructure rivaled Paris.

The American prairie, of course, is a flat, grassy palimpsest upon which cockamamie detritus, such as El Caminos and goat farms, mingles with more modern entanglements, like electric vehicles and strip mall yoga studios. Maybe that's why our dad, never a sentimentalist, didn't stop at the Corn Palace the one time we drove west. Dad knew the tourist trap was just a high school basketball gymnasium where a young Mike Miller swished his free throws. It was also where Dad, back in college in the 1970s, sneaked in with his tuba to play in his college's pep band on bubble-gum chinned bleachers.

"It's just a sweaty gymnasium, boys," Dad said. "We're not stopping for that."

But ennui with the novelty of your own backyard can also be its own oversight. And after my Yankton internship, I'd read that for one week a year, the Corn Palace was the most spectacular whiz-bang concert hall in the West.

***

"Did you ever play the Corn Palace?" I asked Donny, when he sauntered from the C-store that night.

Since starting up the band back in June, I worried about confirming Heather's suspicions around dating a "musician." But if we were going to be the best band in South Dakota, we needed to set our sights on the brightest, most twinkling-marquee-of-a-Terry-Redlin-oil-painting-approved modern-day barn dance venue on the prairie.

Where better than the Corn Palace?

Donny bent low to check the tire pressure, the crooked nose on his face half in shadow, half in the artificial light.

"If they'd pay us," Donny said. "I'll play anything."

His words felt like a quarter—lodged errantly—finally slipped into the jukebox's lodestar, and Johnny Lee's "Looking for Love" lit up blue on the screen. Our van cruised east over that dark highway, our two headlights shining, flashing up a billboard for an associate's degree program in wind turbine repair.

CHAPTER 8

THE UNIVERSITY OF SOUTH DAKOTA

TUESDAY AND WEDNESDAY, JULY 25 AND 26, 2007

I admit, Lawrence Welk's music wasn't for the lorgnette-hoisting crowd.

In *The Rest Is Just Noise*, a history of twentieth-century music, the *New Yorker's* Alex Ross makes absolutely zero references to Lawrence Welk, Myron Floren, big band music, or even Guy Lombardo. The closest he gets is in a section on music during FDR's presidency, noting that Aaron Copland (not the Polka Elvis) supplied Emerson's nearly century-old call for a democratic middlebrow—the intellectualism of the highbrow (Beethoven, Brahms, Shostikovitch) with the capitalistic underpinnings of the lowbrow (salvaging hootenanny tunes).

Fortunately, there are other tomes regarding American music in the twentieth century. For example, Joseph Lanza wrote a book called *Elevator Music: A Surreal History of Muzak, Easy-Listening, and Other Moodsong*, which includes a whopping seventeen references to Welk, even more than Burt Bacharach.

"There are literally 90 million people listening to Muzak per day," Lanza writes.

Which, I mean, I guess.

But that's not to say he didn't receive accolades for his easy-listening, sweet-as-tea music stylings.

In 1939, columnist Cedric Adams wrote in the *Minneapolis Star-Tribune*: "The Northwest should be proud of its extremely personable and talented native son. There are many fine things about Welk's 'Champagned Music,' but to me, the best is that patrons can sit at any table adjacent to the band and still carry on a conversation while the band is playing at its peak."

Just to recap, this is a newspaper reviewer raving about how Welk's band could be both heard and talked over at the same time.

In 1940, the *Kenosha Evening News* noted Welk's music had a "bouncing effect" and expressed regret that "subtler music" such as the kind touted by the Champagne stylists had been "lost in the shuffle when the swing craze took over the country."

Finally, in a cagey review that same year from the *Indianapolis Star,* one Robert G. Tucker accused Welk's band of "resorting every now and then to the barn dance stuff," but begrudgingly acknowledged that Welk's Champagne Orchestra was "considerably out in front of fully 90 percent" of the acts who had barnstormed through Indiana over the previous three or four seasons.

Even the *New York Times* in the 1970s wrote rave reviews of Lawrence Welk's performances at Madison Square Garden (documented in his second, and if I may be honest, slightly disappointing memoir, *Ah-One, Ah-Two*). Although in a book review of *Wunnerful, Wunnerful,* critic Elting E. Morison was more understated.

"It may be that the Champagne Music is to Louis Armstrong as Cliquot Club is to Veuve Cliquot . . . but it works."

There is this belief among Welk's biggest fans, though, that some four-buck-chuck champagne from a bodega's shelf in the heartland was actually exactly what America needed. Fifty-two years after his national TV debut, with the increasingly divided country plunged into two wars across the world, I wondered if America was ready once again for some musical prairie populists.

On that Tuesday afternoon, we rambled into the mildewed, loose-bricked Julian/Brookman dormitory collapsing into the campus at the University of South Dakota for two days of rehearsal.

Monster, as an RA, had a key to an unused classroom. So Donny backed up the SS *Bly* to the picture window, and we unloaded amps, keyboards, drums, and microphone stands into the classroom. Soon cables snaked across the tiled floor.

"We can be as loud as we want till 9 p.m.," assured Monster, scratching at his whiskered chin. "Then Margie shuts us down."

The Brickhouse Boys catalog had been written at the old, black, upright grand piano in the sanctuary of the St. Thomas More Newman Center, where I lived as one of two student residents. At nights, after school. Sometimes in the dark. Me at the piano. Bobby pacing in the pews. I'd pound out an idea, he'd hum a tune. Eventually those melodies—oohs and ahhs echoing out the hallway—grew words. And everything felt dark as a sailor's stout. Moody as an October sunset. The Decemberists-meets-Metallica in a dystopic piano bar. Sometimes Bobby crooned beneath the stained glass, sometimes he shrieked. Once, I snapped a piano string on the note, a sonic bullet bouncing off the walls. But for two weeks, we met almost daily, writing music this way. I'd always written alone, so this felt new, naked. But at the end, when we brought those songs to the band, I had pride, even surprise. We created sounds neither of us could've on our own. Moreover, I realized what power you had in a band when you wrote the music—you had sway, you had your hand on the levers, you communed with the stranger at the door.

So during our two days in Vermillion that late July, I took the helm. Bobby was our band's frontman, no doubt. He's who you watched. But behind the scenes, with the hood up, I could instruct on volume, on slow-downs, or repeating a chorus. I had ideas on Poncho's guitar lick—"more Motown" or "less Steely Dan." And slowly we gelled. We jangled guitars, slapped floor toms, and tinkled stained-glass piano keys playing straight through dinner. We sounded like Radiohead. But we also sounded like Donna Summer. The Strokes. Ben Folds. And Redbone. We sounded like a wedding band stuck in a midwestern indie band's body.

But honestly, at this point, we were also a mess.

Hours later, pooped, we lay supine on the grass, sucking milkshakes from McDonald's.

"God that was a lot of fun," Leo laughed.

But Bobby sat up, dusting grass shards off his Levi's.

"Good bands don't have fun," he reminded us.

This was another rule. Leo straightened up, too.

"Yep," said his brother, Donny. "Hating it is how you get good."

Aesthetically speaking, little overlapped between Welk and us. He played at dances, weddings, and a random attorney's lobby. The Brickhouse Boys, at least until that point, played bars and demolitions of student unions. But developmentally, I saw his shadow in us.

It had been over a year since Bobby and I had written our tranche of original tunes. And I felt, palpably, that a songwriter's only as powerful as his recent hit.

During "This Symphony," Bobby waved his skinny arms to stop the band. The hours grew heavy, made us fussy.

"Are you playing that piano part the same way every time, Chris?"

"Yes," I said breathlessly, "The riff stays the same, man."

On his knobby knees, fidgeting with mousetraps of vocal pedals, Bobby didn't even look up.

"Great," he snapped, "but that's not what I asked you about."

I missed the connotation.

"What a *piano* plays," Bobby continued, "is a *lick*. Guitars play riffs. I asked you about the lick."

The room breathed silence.

Donny wiped his forehead and set down his drumsticks.

"Smoke break," he said, walking out.

I can still stroll down the street singing Welk's band names.

There was the Hotsy Totsy Boys, which sounds more like a group of traveling gas-station service men hired solely to titillate bridesmaids; the Biggest Little Orchestra, impossible to understand whether that's a good thing; and the aspirational Honolulu Fruit

Gum Orchestra, which coincided with a sponsorship deal from a West Coast chewing gum distributor.

On this last score, the band wore colorful leis. During sweaty sets, color bled onto the white shirts. By night's end, his band resembled a flock of Billy Pilgrims, a bunch of sad flamingos.

Willa Cather calls the language of a band its "literature," and that's what I found in Welk—this vernacular antithetical to the dusty prairie.

In 1937, at the William Penn Hotel in Pittsburgh, for example, Lawrence told his national radio audience that he needed a name.

Guy Lombardo and His Royal Canadians, Les Brown and His Duke Blue Devils, and Freddie Fisher and His Schnickelfritzers all had winning handles.

Letters poured in by the stacks. Welk's announcer and office grunt rushed in one morning.

"They're saying that dancing to your music is like sipping champagne. You've got yourself some Champagne Music!"

With Welk's names there was an aspirationalism for a band from the middle of the country. And I knew we needed some dreaminess, too.

By Wednesday evening, the Brickhouse Boys had rehearsed for nearly sixteen hours. In the classroom, Bobby set up a semi-circle of chairs. He grabbed a yardstick and stood near the chalkboard.

"First, let's talk shows."

He slapped the yardstick against the chalkboard, sweat pouring off his forehead.

"Poncho?"

I hoped for Montana, Denver, Seattle. I definitely didn't want to play Fargo/Moorhead.

"We've got a gig in Aberdeen and then two nights in Fargo/Moorhead," Poncho said.

"Good college towns," Donny said.

"*Great* college towns," added Monster.

Next, Bobby ran down the rules.

"First, no going more than two days without a shower or bath."

I nodded, glancing at my brother.

That is okay, his look said back to me.

"Second rule. No leaving your stuff everywhere in the van."

I nodded again at Leo. Reasonable.

"Finally," Bobby said, setting down the yardstick and pacing the room. "If we're going to be the best band in South Dakota, we're going to also get into situations that we wouldn't back at home. So . . ."

Next to me, Leo shuffled his untied sneakers, worriedly.

"What happens on tour stays on tour."

And after paraphrasing the Las Vegas promotional campaign, Bobby turned out the lights.

Dark willows swayed overhead as I hugged the river, turning that phrase over in my head. *What happened on tour, stayed on tour.* What was that—a declarative, an imperative?

And a coldness hit me.

This might not be anything like Lawrence Welk, at all.

That summer, I had read in *South Dakota Magazine* that the bluffs farther north near Chamberlain have been known to emit smoke. If you live in a remote place like that you might say, "Well, at least the land gets me."

But the land didn't get me where I lived.

When I reached the river, soberly I'd texted my friend Collette to meet me by the platform. In minutes, she manifested—with her curly black hair and tennis shoes—out of the forested boardwalk.

"Not thinking about jumping in, are you?" Collette asked.

She had grown up within eyeshot of Mount Rushmore. One of these Black Hills kids, charismatics really. We met our freshman year and stayed friends at the Newman Center, occasionally picking each other off the pavement from various emotional dilemmas.

"Did you get the notes?"

"Yep," she said, "It's pretty impressive stuff."

Tonight, we had business. The "This Day in History" calendar still had dates open.

"Okay, so spring it on me."

She produced a crumpled-up notecard from her jacket's pocket and read by moonlight.

"Apparently the United Nations almost ended up not in New York City, but in . . ."

"Drumroll . . ."

"The Black Hills!"

Collette's eyes were like shiny, bronze buttons.

"Apparently Greece voted for us," Collette sighed, reading off the card before stuffing it back into her pocket. "But the French delegation did not. They said the 'Black Hills' sounded like little piles of dirt."

In part, my draw to Lawrence Welk was the fallacy of proximity. Geography. He inhabited our atmosphere. If I had grown up in Asbury Park, maybe I would've traced down Springsteen's grade school. If eastern Tennessee, probably that old church where Dolly Parton's grandfather preached.

Regardless, I'd become hopelessly attached. We weren't famous people in the rural Midwest. Renown didn't visit flyover country save in a big jetliner or fast car. But one of us had escaped. Grandma told stories of seeing his bands by night's end at the Ritz Ballroom, the dance floor littered in shiny bubblegum wrappers, like silver floorboards.

"I'm not sure about this tour," I told Collette.

The river below us had seemingly lost water elevation over the last few minutes. This could happen in the Dakotas. Whole rivers sucked back into the dirty creek bed in seconds.

"Worried about the cash?"

"No," I said. "I don't think I'm a musician."

An owl may have hooted over our heads, a hawk maybe swooped at a mouse running through the thicket of leaves in a clearing.

Collette sat cross-legged on the wooden planks.

"Chris," she said. "I don't care what you think you are. You need to get out of town. You're just laying in your own bathwater."

The words made my head recoil. I stared at her. Collette loved to pair North Face jackets over North Face sweatshirts and clunky hiking shoes.

"But maybe the band just wants to be some last-ditch spring break trip!" I protested, standing up.

Collette's curly hair blew in the wind, rustling against my face.

"Doesn't mean *you* have to play by those rules."

A big fish *splashed* in the shallow stream. I knew I couldn't stay here.

"Will you call me on tour at least?"

"I'll try," I said. "If we don't get famous."

We walked to the parking lot, and I watched her red taillights float up the side of the bluff, following Dakota Street, back into town.

"Like hills of dirt," I muttered to myself.

Welk had built an empire in this river valley, from a radio tower and barn dances. He had done it from regular folks, in forgotten places. *These were the only rules I needed,* I told myself.

Crawling up the bluff, turning at the gas station, passing by a guy in his early thirties, maybe a PhD student, in a backwards baseball cap, lugging out two sacks of ice with a sixer of beer under the crook of his arm, I once again thought, *maybe we could do it, too.*

Back in my apartment at 123 Forest Avenue, I found my brother fast asleep on the couch. I packed my bag. Socks. A change of shirts. Some jeans. Underwear. Then I stuffed it all down and pressed in my copy of *Wunnerful, Wunnerful.* Without the dust jacket, it was just golden bubbles on the red cover. I figured Welk would be my rabbit's foot, my talisman, a good mentor on the trail.

The very fact that I thought of this bucolic version of Welk reveals how clearly false my view once was of the Champagne Music

Maker. But I didn't know that then. I just kept the window open, my brother's chest rising and falling in the light of the street lantern, and like someone from my family had done for the last 130 years, I slept in the valley of the Missouri River, filled with reeds and catfish and pallid sturgeons, their translucent club heads staring up into what might've been the brightest moon of the last five thousand years.

DANCE #2

A MAZURKA

CHAPTER 9

FALL RIVER COUNTY FAIR IN EDGEMONT, SOUTH DAKOTA

AUGUST 2, 2018

A few nights after our wedding in 2018, Carrie and I scuttled down to a big, old grandstand to watch the rubber check race at the Fall River County Fair. Cowboys rode horses, pushed wheelbarrows, and sprinted through firehoses while locals drank beer and ate barbecue. The orange sun hung over Wyoming's border.

"The homestead was over there," Carrie said, leaning on the guardrail.

A girl with a red cowgirl hat and pigtails swung her legs, looking up.

Combining an assignment for the *Rapid City Journal* with our attempt at a honeymoon, I scoured the grandstand for interview subjects. Dust from the dirt track sparkled in the air. The loudspeaker blasted George Strait.

"People are having fun." I slipped the pen behind my ear and notebook into my pocket. "They don't want an interview."

But Carrie wouldn't give up.

"How about them?"

She pointed to a retired couple. A man with an ergonomic walker sat next to his wife in a pink visor.

We wandered over, and I extended my hand.

"Would you mind being interviewed for the *Journal* about the rubber check race?"

"Wouldn't mind at all," the woman responded. "We've been coming here for years. Custer's gotten suburban. But Edgemont's still wild."

<hr>

I still see the numbers on a laminated cue card.

The Lawrence Welk Show used to get about thirteen million viewers a week at its peak.

Those are *Beverly Hillbillies* numbers. *Ed Sullivan Show* numbers.

And in 1961, at the age of fifty-eight, while the North Dakotan drew a bubble bath in his fancy home with a view of the San Jacinto Mountains, Welk lassoed his first and only number one hit.

"Calcutta," I believe, is the only chart topper to feature a harpsichord prominently. Or, at least, a harpsichord backed by hand claps.

Categorized as "easy listening," there are no words in "Calcutta." There are "oos" and "la-la-las." But no words.

The critic Emily St. James, writing for the *AV Club*, wrote, "Welk didn't want to challenge his audience, really, but he benefited from networks that wanted arts programming and thought he came close enough."

She acknowledges what Welk wanted most was to throw a "fizzy party that would never end."

Cue "Calcutta."

The song is not bad. It's breezy, catchy, like the background music to an old commercial for a Volkswagen spinning along pigtail roads somewhere over lush Ibiza.

But the song's genius is not the American cornfield Svengali, but the midcentury German pop artist Heino Gaze.

In 1958, Gaze took "Calcutta on the Ganges" to the top of the charts in his home country. His song appears to be exactly like Welk's, save there are lyrics, with the crooner naming a series of rivers and the cities upon them. Oh, and Madeleine. His love for Madeleine. The lyrics go like this:

Calcutta lies on the Ganges
Paris is on the Seine
But I'm so in love
It's up to Madeleine

And then we repeat, with new towns, new bodies of water: New York and the Atlantic, Congo's Nile, London and the Thames, etcetera. Throw in a key change, some artisanal accordion, and you have a hit.

A graduate student with an interest in postcolonialism might make hay here of this German singer's fascination with former imperial ports, a gallivanting westerner feting his paramour by jetliner from one cosmopolitan city to another with lusty "yips."

But it's also a song about love.

Since yesterday she loves, too,
just me and my geography

A couple years ago, I asked my friend, Altman Studeny, at Haskett's Café in downtown Sioux Falls, to explain "Calcutta."

The song was bracketed on the Cash Box 100 charts in late winter 1961 by "Will You Love Me Tomorrow" from the Shirelles (by way of Carole King), and the union-hall-rocking "Pony Time" by the inimitable Chubby Checker.

"It's those insipid hand claps, Christopher," Altman told me, over a salad. "They're the ticket."

A South Dakota art professor with thick, black glasses who also served on the city council for his hometown of Plankinton, Altman moonlighted as the announcer for the local American Legion baseball games, where he often played a between-innings soundtrack through tin speakers dangling from wooden light poles comprising Jackson 5's "I Want You Back" and Fleetwood Mac's "Don't Stop" (Mick Fleetwood's jaunty floor-tom chop was always a pick-me-up for the Pirates) and, on moodier nights, perhaps when Altman had learned the second basemen suffered from a little teenage love blues, even "Sundown" by the Canadian song-poet Gordon Lightfoot, which would echo hauntingly all the way to Al's I-90 gas stop.

Those tunes rarely earned more than a few foot taps.

But whenever Altman played "Calcutta," which sounds like a white wine spritzer finished off by Ricky Nelson swinging his microphone, the short-cropped moms opened Capri Suns on the aluminum bleachers, bobbing their heads, while the dads chewing and spitting out Dakota sunflower seeds quietly nodded. Maybe the Coca-Cola cans opened with a more enthusiastic *crack-splash*.

"Kitsch is participatory," Altman will say. "You can't help but want to join in on the fun . . . even if you don't want to."

On that hot, dusty day in Edgemont, 1,500 miles from an ocean, I took out my notebook and phone to record the interview.

"Frank used to teach band out in Pine Ridge," his wife said.

"Never thought a Chicago boy would end up out here," said Frank.

"Fantastic!" Carrie exclaimed, turning to me. "You can use that in your story, right, Christopher?"

I sat down, a can of Coca-Cola at my feet, the interview mostly over after the Custer quote.

"How'd you end up out here?" I asked. "What's the story?"

"We met in college," the wife said. "At Dakota Wesleyan."

Then Frank grinned, the sunset reflecting off his copper sunglasses.

"I learned how to play the C-sharp saxophone from Lawrence Welk's saxophonist," he said.

I sat up.

"Excuse me?"

As St. James writes, "Watching the early episodes of *The Lawrence Welk Show*—before the series was overwhelmed by the cheesy musical skits that dominate the program in the public imagination—is watching a culture struggling to hold onto itself in the face of a coming youth movement."

Back in the mid-1930s, when Welk discovered the Novachord organ, he got accused by some reviewers of imposing a hot "electric" sound on listeners.

Once, Deadwood hotelier Bill Walsh, who grew up in Mitchell, told me he and his high school buddies parked cars on nights Welk's orchestra came to town to play the World's Only Corn Palace.

"We had to invent new places, son."

***

Over the cowbells and country music, I leaned into Frank's story, probing questions.

"He only had one female musician during his whole career," Frank said, "But she taught saxophone at Dakota Wesleyan. And I was her student!"

The smell of horses and livestock hung in the air, but I didn't think any B.S.

As Carrie and I walked out to our car, past the beer cans—mostly the cheap ones with the blue labels discarded into the tubs—I wanted to rehear the sentence's music.

She taught me the C-sharp saxophone.

That night, Wyoming swallowing up the sun and returning a moon sliver high above the granite peaks of the southern Hills, we drove into the foothills, dappled every once in a while with a pine tree, or an ATV, or piano, or faded "MAGA" flags, or one of those accordions collecting dust.

CHAPTER 10

THE YAPATORIUM IN ABERDEEN, SOUTH DAKOTA

THURSDAY, JULY 26, 2007

On that last Thursday morning in July, my brother Leo and I waited in frayed jean shorts aside Forest Avenue when the *Bly* rumbled down the street.

Bobby stuck his head out the window.

"Get in, losers!"

The neighborhood pulled tight its blinds. Mothers clutched children tight to their waists. Dogs shivered with leashes wrapped around porch posts.

We threw our packs in the open sliding door and stepped in. Then we rumbled off, a trail of exhaust in our wake.

Lawrence Welk, too.

On his twenty-first birthday, Lawrence woke early, dressed, checked on his valise ("my small hoard of money"), smoothed out his quilt, and joined the family for breakfast, ready to leave them for good.

"He'll be back in six weeks looking for a good meal!" Ludwig joked.

Ludwig had never seen eye-to-eye with Lawrence, especially on the boy's dream. Partly this was fear of inheritance. The Welks had an ancestor, a blind man in rags, who had wandered the countryside back in Prussia, double-jointed, playing the accordion for money, sleeping in cow pastures and bird-poop-stained stone aviaries just to make a living.

To Ludwig, the man had been a joke, a punch line, and the elder Welk hadn't sailed to America with Christine and dragged a dispassionate ox and a Bible one hundred miles to see his son fetter away prosperity on a squeezebox.

But while his family laughed at Ludwig's joke, Lawrence just swallowed his pride and shook his father's hand, noting an "ending and a beginning" in his memoir.

And then he made his way out of the house.

"Lawrencell," his mother whispered in the German tongue, tearfully.

Turning around, her boy kissed her on the cheek, grabbed his accordion, and hopped into the buggy. Every few yards, he writes, he turned and saw his mother standing by the clothesline, waving and waving, her figure getting smaller and smaller and smaller.

⸻

The Brickhouse Boys drove north along I-29 on that Thursday afternoon, the prairie wind passing through Donny's open window, fluttering the collection of Doritos bags at our feet. At Sioux Falls, we peeled into the Guitar Center. Standing in the parking lot, as I had suspected, were my parents.

"It's my fault," said Leo. "I didn't know where else to send the shirts." The band tiptoed into the big box music store, and we trudged over.

I know it wasn't cool for parents to show up on tour. But my brother had decided to ship the T-shirts (our "merchandise") to our parents' house in Wells, Minnesota, so at the simplest request, they had driven over, now complicit in trafficking our longshot dreams.

"These look pretty snazzy," Mom called out, using her teacher's voice.[1]

Dad was less impressed. "Whose idea for shirts was this? You think people will actually buy these?"

Mom wore a wide hat and Dad stood in boxy, cargo shorts, looking more prepared for boarding a boat to photograph whales in a fjord than picking up after the grown boys.

The T-shirts were Bobby's idea, in my defense. After blazing through Hunter S. Thompson's paperbacks, purloined from a thrift store earlier that year, Bobby asked that the writer's face appear on our shirts along with the tag, "One more band for Gonzo."

"These were intentional?" asked our father.

Leo opened up the cardboard box to find every T-shirt in a different size. A "medium" draped down to my 6-foot-4-inch brother's knees.

"I mean, it was the cheapest place I could find on the Internet," he reasoned. "Some guy in New Jersey. Can't really complain."

Our father smirked, sipping his Diet Coke.

"Should we talk about your night at the opera house?"

Leo looked confused.

"The Queen album?"

"No, *your* night there in Wessington Springs."

And I panicked.

This was another rule—for Welk and us—to say goodbye to parents.

Weeks earlier we played Angus's birthday party at the opera house in Wessington Springs, and a man did, it was true, climb on stage in just his briefs. It was also true that, reciprocally, Bobby threw off his T-shirt and jeans and sang in his Batman briefs. Worse, this was all captured on video and uploaded to YouTube, so when you searched "Brickhouse Boys," which I'm sure our parents had been doing on a weekly basis, the first link up was a blurry, night-vision camera video of two mostly naked men dancing on an opera house stage.

But they couldn't blame the bystanders.

---

1. Which often meant she was covering over a difficult truth with a separate, expedient observation and air of breeziness.

"That wasn't *us*," I said. "That was *Bobby* and, some, some guy."

"Do you think that was cool?" Dad replied. "Is that what kind of band you're in?"

My brother, normally forbearing, scoffed.

We'd now created a scene in the Sioux Falls Guitar Center parking lot (likely not the first).

Mercifully, Mom intervened.

"Boys," she said, using her teacher's voice, her eyes hidden behind wide, black sunglasses. "When we saw James Taylor in concert, he wore just a baseball cap, T-shirt, and jeans. And, he played beautifully for two hours. That's all he needed. That's all you need. Let your music do the talking for you."

Five minutes later, humiliated, we drove across town only to plunge into a thrift store to pick up our uniforms.

"We want to look like old-school milkmen," Bobby said, brazenly.

"With pink ascots," said Monster, clutching a roll of pink fabric he found near the horse-themed carpet squares.

So we rummaged the women's section, finding all-white trousers and blouses to make David Bowie proud. But when Leo and I stepped up to pay, my brother gasped as the guys walked out—with our merchandise balled up in Poncho and Donny's pants—straight through the double-doors.

"They probably would've given this to us for free," Leo whispered, below the clerk's preying eye.

To be a college graduate and abetting shoplifting for the first time only compounded my dour mood.

But I could also see that our ties to Welk were only growing stronger. The uniforms, while hodgepodge, cleaned us up, just like Welk's own three-piece-suited band dazzled on stage, I thought. Secondly, we already—like Welk—had a dance band sound, with my piano and Danny's drums aided by my brother's insistence on laying down a disco bass for every tune, even while playing in a haybale opera house.

And finally, perhaps most fatalistically, Welk, too, like us, was headed to the Hub City.

"I had gone to Aberdeen, South Dakota, the day I left the farm," he writes to open the second section of *Wunnerful, Wunnerful,* which I opened up again as we blew north on the interstate, "partly because we had friends living there, and partly because I had only enough money to buy a ticket that far."

Aberdeen back then was a town of fifteen thousand people who eagerly awaited a boom that never came. In the 1880s, four railroads converged in the prairie metropolis. They were still waiting for the operas and baseball teams and movie theaters.

Fortunately, his parents wouldn't be around.

"Nobody was ever as dumb as I!" he writes, observing he joined a for-profit children's choir.

"I was two feet taller and ten years older than anybody else in the group," Welk explains, "But I didn't care. I was earning money and gaining experience, and I just beamed and smiled right along with the other members of the Jazzy Junior Five."

Reaching the Hub City's outskirts, I wondered if the dandy gentle-manliness of those early years had faded. Strip malls, Burger Kings, big trucks with dastardly tailpipes.

"Keep your eye out for the Yapatorium," yelled Donny, cutting across a gas station parking lot to save time at a red light.

Eventually, we rolled up to a cheerless brick schoolhouse, anchored by an American flag and a young woman in cutoffs and sunglasses, leaning against a stop sign, boasting a tattoo of what appeared to be a lake leviathan crawling up her right arm.

"You come for the show?" asked Bobby, leaning out the window.

The woman flashed her eyebrows behind the pink sunglasses.

"Nah," she said. "I'm working parole."

The cocksure attitude we had as a rambling, British prog-rock band from the '70s pulling into a dusty cow town evaporated.

"You guys playing?" she asked. "You look a little old?"

My brother, embarrassedly, dug into his *Harry Potter.* But Bobby, who even at twenty-years-old was already a veteran of the touring life, was like a sailor catching a face full of brackish seawater.

"Our band's just getting started," he said. "We probably could use the practice."

Kara shrugged her shoulders as if to say, *your problem, not mine.* Then she threw her cigarette on the ground and, her hips like two upside-down treble clefs pressed palindromically together, pushed off the flagpole and ambled back toward the brick school.

Sitting silently, Bobby slowly turned from the front seat.

"Remember rule number three. What happens on tour *stays* on tour."

The night's show, like the gig in Pierre, didn't feel like the opening salvo of a band trying to get famous.

Bobby tore off his shirt, Monster's flimsy keyboard fell, knocking out another key from its hockey mouth, and Donny—angry he had to work that night back in Sioux Falls's UPS warehouse—slammed his drumsticks on the snare at song's end.

"Sorry, everybody. I forgot to mention how much we suck!"

But the night belonged to the headliners anyway. The lead singer of this Miami band jumped onto a guitar amp and launched into a tirade about international politics.

"My father worked in Pinochet's cabinet," he yelled.

The kids below the stage raised up hands, in chaotic rhythms.

"Do you know about Pinochet?!" Buzzer shouted.

A variety of vague responses came in shouts.

While the singer yelled out Pinochet's treatment of political prisoners, the guitarist scratched his fretboard, like a large pterodactyl rapidly descended toward prey. I stood flat-footed in back of the cafeteria, as Monster counted our cash receipts from T-shirt sales.

Launching off the bass drum onto the floor, the singer turned his attention locally.

"I've heard about you, South Dakota," he cried. "And I've heard about your Indians!"

Welk's hometown of Strasburg, North Dakota, sits thirty miles east— and across the Missouri River—from Fort Yates, the tribal headquarters of the Standing Rock Sioux Reservation—though he never mentions the Lakotas in any of his books.

Part of that, due to segregation, is the road. There is no direct road to get to Standing Rock, whittled down from the Great Sioux Reservation. Of course, that's no mistake. In 1887, at the tail-end of the Dakota Land Boom, Congress passed the Dawes Act, breaking the treaties and winnowing land. Two years later, Standing Rock was partitioned off. Two years after that, Ludwig and Christine Welk—from eastern Europe—arrived with their Bible, ox, and accordion.

As far as I can tell, there is only one book with Welk's name on the cover in which he talks about the Oceti Sakowin: a biography. In 1957's *Mister Music Maker*, author Mary Lewis Coakley gives Welk's ties to the Lakota real estate. Coakley writes that Welk used to pull up the quilt at night with "boyish imagination" and almost hear whoops of nearby Sioux returning home after a "drinking spree."

It's the imagination I think about. Did boyish mean innocent?

In the 1880s, L. Frank Baum, living in the Hub City, would drink up the frontier that would inspire the frame narrative for his later work, *The Wizard of Oz*. Baum published a newspaper, and after the massacre at Wounded Knee in 1890, he opined that the Sioux should be "exterminated" from the land.

You wonder if this was imagination, too. Or a failure of imagination.

Maybe imagination needs to grow up. "Boyish" is a plastic bow and arrow. "Boyish" is a headdress on a hockey fan in a Grand Forks arena. "Boyish" is the grocer up the road in Linton, North Dakota, who in 2016 told the *Fargo Forum* with enthusiasm how the oil pipeline's construction helped the bags of chip and bottles of pop keep flying off the shelves.

"What about these second-class citizens?" cried the singer, balling up his fist. "What about incarceration rates? About racism?"

He wasn't wrong in his facts. But the crowd knew the see-no, hear-no, speak-no rule of the prairie. It was easier to gin up kids' anger at outrage two thousand miles away rather than in their own backyard, and the teenagers slowed down. Feet dragged. Fewer punches popped up into the air.

They couldn't imagine oppression. It surrounded them, which means they could forget it, explain it, rationalize it.

By set's end, the singer fastened the microphone back on the stand, as kids filed in line for city-paid juice boxes and video game tickets.

"Thanks," he said, wiping sweat off his forehead. "We've got merch in back."

I burst through the double doors into the dark night, air cold against my skin. Across the long, flat pavement, a man in a white T-shirt walked out onto his porch, with a light on, bugs humming in the glow, reading a magazine.

According to his memoir, the "dancing public" was slim back in Aberdeen, so after a few weeks Lawrence trains to Bismarck, North Dakota, a city he calls the "most exciting city I'd seen thus far."

Bismarck doesn't work out, either.

Basically, Lawrence is scandalized by its progressivism.

"It was in Bismarck," he writes, "that I first learned there was such a thing as divorce, and I was shocked."

Apparently, he worked as a piano salesman, sold zero pianos, and failed to produce gigs. So, Lawrence trained back to Aberdeen for junior choirs and a more traditional definition of marriage.

That night in Aberdeen, Bobby ran off with Kara, and Donny's girlfriend, Kris, drove from Sioux Falls to take him to work at UPS because, like the rest of us, Donny was pretty broke, too. Leo, Monster, Poncho, and I fended for ourselves in the Hub City.

Vinny, the promoter, stood nervously near the doorway, watching for any juice-box thievery.

"Hey, do you have a place my band could stay?" I asked.

This was my secondary goal on tour—to avoid vagrancy.

Vinny looked business-like, as if he'd been sitting on a back-up plan for years.

"I always wonder where you guys stay. Most bands never ask."

Within minutes, we were in the *Bly*, driving downtown, past old homes bearing those imperturbable faces mentioned in Joyce's "Araby," and after crossing a gas station, we spotted the hulking Victorian mansion Vinny described.

A beer pong party in full play on the first floor. In a stairwell of the dilapidated home stood a skinny, dark-complexioned kid in a yellow stocking cap waving to us.

"Come on up, dudes," Kyle yelled. "Don't mind the rabble-rousers below."

Welk has this pithy line early in his book, referencing sleeping in a stranger's house on the road, saying, "those being the days when people trusted each other." But his faith in yesterday's trustworthiness often, somehow, felt vaguely cynical.

With Poncho sleeping in the van, Leo, Monster, and I climbed up the narrow, winding, wooden stairs to the top, where this stranger stood smiling, welcoming us into his spacious apartment.

His walls glimmered in colorful canvases.

"These yours, man?" asked Monster.

"Yeah," Kyle said, sheepishly.

"You sell 'em? Locally?" I asked.

"I got some offers from back home in Sisseton," said Kyle. "But you know, when I paint for my people, they can't afford my stuff. And when I paint for people who *can* afford my stuff, it's not for *my* people, you know?"

Hungry, we walked across the street to the sit under the bug-covered lights on the curb, eating rubbery hot dogs from the gas station, watching cars stream past.

"What's 'making it' mean to you all?" asked Kyle.

"Maybe a gig that pays?" said Poncho, whom we'd rousted from slumber.

"Get rid of my college debt," said Monster.

"Playing the Corn Palace," I said.

Heads rotated my way.

My brother wiped a slab of mustard from his cheek.

"Do they even do shows?"

"They do," said Kyle. "I saw Britney Spears there in the sixth grade. It was magical. I put her poster on my wall."

Monster, still wearing his dress shoes, balanced on the curb like a concrete pommel horse. A streetlamp flared his cheekbones.

"First we got to survive tomorrow night's show."

"Where's tomorrow's show?" asked my brother.

Monster rolled up his hotdog tinfoil into a ball and chucked it into a dumpster, flies hovering overhead.

"You don't want to know."

An IROC cruised past, with Kara driving and Bobby in the front seat.

"I'll see you boys tomorrow!" Bobby called.

It felt like a dream, but as Kara navigated the intersection on a sharp right turn, the tire squeals engulfed his mantra.

"Singers," said Kyle. "That's why I just ride solo."

***

Going on tour felt like entering a new subterranean world, beneath the catacombs, swimming under a lake only to pop up in a dark limestone cave. Or, like, how rain forests come alive at night. I had left the realm of internships and regular mass attendance and the carpet of the library's study rooms to enter this frenzied forest of late-night pizza delivery guys quoting Joan Didion or a band just off a gig in East Los Angeles who told you about parties and all-night burrito stands and invited you out for a winter show. Large highways invisible to most regular folks illuminated at night, stretching across the country for a traveling musician, and I sensed the thrill of escape, of rebirth.

That night, Kyle gave us pillows for our sleeping bags, and Leo and I rolled out on his living room floor, when a pulsing blue washed over my cell phone.

And I placed my hand over it, heart bass-drumming.

Earlier that summer, in mid-June, I'd gotten a text message from Heather, reading, "I love you, pup! I'm so proud of you." My chest had filled with a rush of euphoria. Had she'd heard I was going to be a musician? Did she want me back? But then I'd gazed at the time-stamp and read: May 12, 2007. 10:03 a.m. My graduation day. Somehow the text message had gotten lost in space, sent around Saturn's rings, and boomeranged back. I remember staring at the letters, flickering like little ghosts, confusing past and present.

I lifted the cell phone, but it was only Mom.

"Call in the morning to talk about show?" she'd texted. "Hope you sold T-shirts."

I was on my way. Feeling the breeze carry in through the window, off the faraway hills, the Tetons, the Cascades, the Pacific, I wondered how many musicians over the years had been in this town, passing through, trying to sleep on floors, like me, listening to the sounds of drifting-by cars driven by men, going up and down the highway, looking for gas stations or fast foods still open before they, too, eventually, returned home.

CHAPTER 11

THE NESTOR TAVERN IN FARGO, NORTH DAKOTA

FRIDAY, JULY 27, 2007

From the factory speakers of the SS *Bly* that summer, radio broadcasts occasionally interrupted our otherwise myopic musical campaign.

Airstrikes in Baghdad.

Bear Stearns liquidating some hedge funds.

Presidential candidates barnstorming neighboring Iowa.

But these dispatches felt so distant. I could look at a map and trace the 1,600 or so miles between Aberdeen and Hollywood—the same distance that existed one hundred years prior. But events somehow felt farther. An earthquake had opened up craters in the land, split apart the terra firma, making the old route impassable. Certainly, quick channels—portals, really—for men and women our age existed to Afghanistan. Friends talked of fishing boats in Alaska for jobs. But we were farther than ever from New York City or Los Angeles.

So, instead, we became consumed with the narcissism of the statewide scene. Rock bands, after all, at least the more rural ones, metamorphize with geology. They reveal the land they grew up in. Especially in South Dakota, where acoustics, like saltwater baths or fog off a bluestem savannah, roil up from below.

The state's eastern half consists of land flattened by a glacier. Such topographical ennui has spurred groups like the Red Willow

Band, pearl-button buskers from the 1970s, or Snakebeard Jackson, an *O Brother Where Art Thou*-inspired troupe of luthiers. Flatness made for big dreams. With little sonic diversity.

Out west, it gets stranger.

In the central part of the state, the land bubbles up into barren, grassy hills along which the Missouri splits the state in two. A few punk and metal bands fly off stages into empty crowds around Midland, Phillip, Kadoka, Fort Pierre, tiny towns with pickled hardboiled eggs in jars reposing on wooden counters. There hasn't been a paying gig out here since the Mesozoic era.

No one plays the Badlands—those vampiric stone castles—either, save for loners who bust acoustic guitars out the back of their Volkswagen van on cross-country road trips at the gas station in Interior as in Chloe Zhao's *The Rider*.

I once spoke with Brady Jandreau, the Lakota rodeo star who, in Zhao's film, trains horses and attempts to heal himself. He patted the broad hindside of a brown mare, whispering her name, telling her she was a good girl, and then he told me the national press tours—Terry Gross's *Fresh Air*, the BBC, the *New York Times*—had gotten weird eventually.

"Folks just don't understand people like me," he said.

"Like how?" I asked, holding up my microphone.

"People who eat and ride animals."

Finally are the Black Hills. Music here looks more like Denver, like Missoula, where wild-eyed mountain bands yelp at the piney moon. Country bands playing psychedelic rock. Indigenous hip hop stars. I once descended into an English basement tavern in Deadwood where a cowpunk band raged. Later, I saw an emcee rapping in the Buffalo, adjacent to where Wild Bill had been shot in the back of the head. She bobbed her head before slipping into a moonwalk.

In some spots, music—like geysers—seeps up from the earth.

It was some newer, more unnatural erosion catching my attention, though, as we traipsed across the Dakotas in 2007.

Cruising east on Highway 212 for Fargo the next morning, blue sky draped over us like a tarp. A yellow sun hung high, and white birds dove into the adjacent blue lakes. Bobby drove, sipping gas station coffee from a Styrofoam cup, while Leo pulled the beekeeper's hat over his face to sleep. In back, Monster leisurely crossed his thin, hairy legs over Poncho's cooler, re-reading *Post Office*. I watched the countryside, trying to place a scene from *Wunnerful, Wunnerful.*

On a morning back in 1925, Welk waltzed into an Aberdeen Chevrolet dealership, kicked some tires, ran his hands along the fenders, and asked the man the price of this beautiful touring car.

"$700, son."

Welk had wanted a touring car. He had marshaled an orchestra. But he was short by about $700. So he offered to mention the dealership at the gigs in exchange for zero down.

The dealer twisted his mustache, then stuck out his hand.

"You throw a pretty good deal there, young man."

And, as prophesied by Boz Scaggs, Welk drove it off the lot.

But could that still happen?

I stared out the window. There was just a nagging resistance to this euphoria.

Rust-peppered pickups eased off dirt roads and boarded-up farmhouses. Giant babies hovered over the air in stained pro-life billboards. Bustling main streets crammed into Morton steel buildings housing the movie rental, groceries, post-office, and bar out by the highway. Posters nailed to windows advertised the benefit supper or the for-sale feeder.

At the I-29 truck-stop, Leo and I got out to inspect the Mello Yellos and ran into a T-shirt of a dog carrying a pheasant in its jaws. The logo said: "A Bitch Looks Best with a Cock in Her Mouth."

"Must be a family store," Leo said.

After returning from a longstanding gig with the broke Lincoln Boulds and His Famous Chicagoans and buying up that car, Lawrence carried a hefty debt around his neck.

So he set up his Fourth of July dance at Scatterwood Lake.

"We all loved those Fourth of July celebrations," Lawrence wrote, perhaps while sitting in his El Mirador home in Palm Springs, feet tugging the shag carpet, green eyes looking out onto the neon pool, a ginger ale on ice within reach on the powder-blue pedestal sink of his old hands as he talked into a Dictaphone.

Welk calls the locals the "most American Americans" he'd ever known.

Scatterwood Lake Pavilion was a twinkling carousel of a dance hall, with Christmas lights, latticed arches, and a wide, wooden dance floor roped off in the center.[1] The rule in those days was that patrons paid a nickel for three spins. Afterward, ushers cleared the floor with a long, velvet rope.

"People were so used to this procedure that the ropes were not really necessary," Lawrence writes with the assistance of that equestrian coach, Bernice McGeehan, "but it was part of the scene of the day."

The scene of the day.

Within an hour, the *Bly*, carrying six musicians and their instruments, pilgrimaged into Fargo traffic, dipped under a train track elevated by heavy cinders, and rolled up to the Nestor Tavern.

"Whoa," Leo said from the back. "We're playing *here*?"

A shoebox, windowless bar capped with a green awning, the Nestor sat surrounded by a pool of parking lot just off downtown Fargo. In the entranceway, a woman in a Canadian tuxedo tossed off ashes and yelled at a kid.

"You're at your Dad's tonight!"

Waves of heat squiggled from the hot concrete. From a grease trap oozed spoiled fruit smells. A trucker worked on his cab.

We had played some tough spots, but I paused before unlatching the *Bly*'s side door.

---

1. In the summer of 2016, I visited and found a weeded-over cemetery, an old gravel road bifurcating a cattle farm next to a grassy beach running alongside a quiet lake.

"Not going to look any less stupid outside than in," said Donny. So in we went.

The dankness enveloped us immediately.

At the microphone, a man in a wheelchair called out bingo numbers to muffled "harrumphs" and clinks of beer bottles. On the diamonded dance floor at a card table a woman with an oxygen tank yammered loudly about the price of milk and some celebrity wedding. Her friends stared at their cards. The stars-and-bars pattern was superimposed over a faded beer clock. Groups of leather jackets yelled by the pool tables while a jukebox carried the impression Junior was the only denomination of the name Hank Williams worth knowing.

"Was this the only venue available?" I whispered to Poncho.

"Yeah, man," our guitarist said, wiping his brow. "Be my guest, though. Plenty of places downtown."

In the back of the dark bar, a vertical rectangle of white light illuminated the doorway. Out that, awaited downtown.

I dashed off.

If Welk—barely knowing English—could wrangle an audience in Hague, so could we land a fallback gig a century later in this cowtown.

Racing in view of the old *FORUM* marquee, I ducked into the first bar. But the bartender just shook his head, wiping down the counter.

"We just do acoustic,"

Frustrated, I went next door.

"Johnny's got someone for tonight," said the hostess. "Sorry, but tomorrow or next weekend?"

"Nah," I said, panic like bile rising in my throat. "We're from South . . . ahh, just nevermind."

Finally, I spotted a joint called "The Aquarium" that had a stacked music calendar with bands from Minneapolis pasted to the wall.

"Hey," I excitedly said to the woman behind the glass in the lobby. "How do I get on a bill with my band?"

She looked up, amused.

"Like for tonight?"

I nodded.

She had purple hair and a nose piercing.

"Oh, honey, we're booked three months out."

"Here's Chuck's number," she said, handing me a card. "Give him a call."

I stuffed the card in my back pocket, turned in the direction of the Nestor, and walked.

Halfway there, I spied a lanky man standing under a billboard for a dentist, the giant man's eyes fried from overexposure.

"You get us a show?!" my brother called, waving a Mello Yello.

I shook my head.

"Shooooot," Leo called, reflectively taking a sip and screwing back on the cap. "Whole place just smells bad in there."

"Like what?" I asked. "Cigarettes?"

"Like a pet store," Leo said.

We ducked back to the bar, and I ordered an amaretto sour.

It wasn't fair. In Welk's world, dancers showed up early. Families ate fried chicken, corn-on-the-cob, watermelon. Children terrorized the countryside with sparklers. The *clop-clop-clop* of horses lent a festive, happy scene to the lake. But here I was with a stuffed bobcat on the wall snarling at me.

"What you reading, cowboy?"

I looked up. The bartender had freckles and blonde hair.

I put my hands over my copy of *Wunnerful, Wunnerful*.

"Nothing," I said. "Say, you ever have any violence break out here?"

She jousted toothpicks into olives.

"No one's hurting anyone that ain't got it coming."

I took a swig of the yellow, sugary drink. "That's reassuring, thanks." A toilet flushed from the nearby men's room, a *crack* of pool balls.

"You boys gonna have a good crowd tonight," she said.

Her hands pressed the towel into the bar, and she leaned over, a silver charm necklace dangling from her neck, as someone put a dollar in to hear a song. It sounded like George Jones but with a woman's voice.

Can I have this dance—for the rest of my life?
Would you be my partner—every night?

"There's a tune," she said. "Anne Murray."

She stabbed the last olive.

"My daddy loved this song."

Looking around the Nestor, what worried me was whether this crowd—tough, scuffed hands and faces weathered like old baseball glove mitts—would take kindly to a band like ours.

But I had forgotten the common law of country music: melody knows no boundaries.

"Here's the deal," the bartender said, leaning on her elbows on the flat surface, the spaghetti straps of her blue tank top stretching over her bare shoulders, her blonde bun loosely tied. "You've got to be authentic."

"Like John Prine?" I asked.

"Like Prine," she nodded. "Or Hank III. Or, shoot, like Liberace or DMX. I don't really care about aesthetics. Just, you know, be you."

"Got it," I said.

"And if anyone gives you lip, just look my way."

What I like most about the Scatterwood Pavilion scene is that for once, Lawrence faced a dilemma just like ours.

He was trapped.

As the dance's kickoff approached, all the families mysteriously left. Lawrence raised his baton for the opening number, and only three couples twirled on the big dance floor.

"Oh, you know, it's the county championship game," one dancer said, to the panicked conductor, when pressed for a reason for the exodus. "Everybody's there."

Lawrence's hopes slammed to the hardwood floor.

No band could out-pull the local nine men. Not even Mr. Lawrence Welk and his Hotsy Totsy Boys.

"I was angry at myself for not looking more fully into the situation and angrier at the owner for not telling me," he fumes.

The opening band—a bunch of shirtless guys doing '90s alt-rock—threw a CD release party. After a trio of songs, the lead singer yelled out, "Get your butts up here! Support local musicians!"

Wild yelps went up behind me, but only because on the television, Joe Mauer hit a homerun. Mullets and do-rags and faded ball caps with Air Force numbers filled the joint. Leo, in his beekeeper's hat, only nineteen, manifested at my shoulder.

"We should change."

We grabbed our bags and walked into the men's room. Stripped to our boxers, we stepped into white, women's pants picked up from Saver's, when a guy entered in wearing cowboy boots and a Sturgis shirt.

"Whoa, whoa, whoa," he said. "This ain't New York City!?"

"I know," my brother shot, from behind the john's door. "We hear ya."

"You're in F-A-R-G-O."

The man whizzed into the alabaster stall and washed up.

I fastened the tight pants and buttoned up the white blouse to my throat. Tying on the pink ascot, I saw myself in the graffiti mirror—tall, sideburns, blue eyes, brown scraggly hair and about fifteen pounds lighter than I started the summer.

"You look like a deranged candy man," Leo said.

"They're going to punish us, aren't they?" I muttered.

The door slammed open, as we braced for another geographical treatise. But it was only Monster, waving Mickey Mouse gloves.

"It's time, boys."

As Lawrence listlessly waved his baton, he didn't even notice the large thunderclouds rolling in from the western skies. A few drops of rain splashed outside the pavilion. Then, a few families—with damp hair—sprinted under the big top. Others under the trees. Then a crescendo of sprinkles.

The baseball umpire held up his arm, analyzing the threat.

And a dopey smile crossed our polka maestro's face when he realized what was up, his wrist vigorously picking up tempo.

Admittedly, the classical-style piano melody to open "Apathy" did little to dissuade the hecklers up front.

"Play some Metallica!"

"Sing me a song, piano-man!"

Most of the patrons, mercifully, ignored us.

But while I could play the piano like a music box, I could push it like a tackling sled, too. I could play my piano like a horse you lead out of danger, tensing your legs, pulling the reins close. My right hand, in *ritardando*, slowly decelerated. My pinky finger tapped the highest, gentlest note on the piano, and like a silver scissors snipping the rope, the song transitioned from introduction to the non-classical verse, and the piano hurtled with deadening speed toward the sidewalk.

SMASH!

Splinters everywhere.

The audience at Scatterwood exploded. Thunder *cracked*, *boomed*.

Crowds of people fled onto the safe harbor of the dry dance floor, nickels and dimes rolling over the counter.

Lawrence, at least according to his own memoir, was on his way.

Under the rain, his band tweeted and tooted and rip-roared with increased oomph. In a climactic moment, his former adversaries, the soggy baseball team, in full regalia, stumbled into the arena.

Soon, the owner sheepishly walked past, calling out, "Made a pretty good deal for yourself, young fella."

Lawrence didn't respond. The owner hadn't told Welk about the baseball game. So the maestro just smiled and kept twirling the baton as the red-roped ushers worked double-time into the night.

The walls of that little bar in downtown Fargo throbbed. The roof shook. Donny's drums, like a wave, rushed in. Leo held his bass as confidentially as a proton pack. Poncho's fingers fluttered on the guitar. Even Monster on this night pat-a-panned his tambourine on his polyester thigh, holding down the organ, while Bobby's voice hit like the taxidermied wildcat come to life, howling in the night, and that bar turned to our little band on the forgotten stage.

> *Horse whips and chains!*
> *Steel cage, I'm trained!*
> *It's just a classic rope-a-dope!*

The skullcaps, Vietnam hats, gold teeth, oxygen tanks, pretty young misses, denim queens, rusted Pony Boys, and man in a wheelchair gravitated to the stage, crushing toward us and stretching back to the pool tables, where a grinning, wild-eyed, mischievous Puck hung atop a ladder or a tree or a bar stool, staring at the boys in white kimonos punching out on stage, nodding their heads and stomping boots.

When I looked up, by the first chorus, the bartender bare arms akimbo, towel on her shoulder, smiled wide at me, giving me a thumbs-up before sliding another gin-and-soda down the bar to a patron.

At bar close, water pooled in the potholes like small ponds. A pickup peeled out near the grain bins. We stood under the green awning, rain falling, as the bands shared cigarettes, and I spied the bartender walking home underneath the raised train tracks. Before leaving, she told me that we played better than Spill Canvas, a Sioux Falls band that had their poster draped in New York City's Times Square.

"What a ride, man," said my brother. "I just feel like going on a trip. Don't you?"

Leo meant like a road trip to the Red River, to howl under the moon. But the opening band's guitarist overheard and made a simple, if predictable, homonymic error.

"*Trip?*" he asked. "I can get shrooms or acid. What do you need?"

CHAPTER 12

A RAMBLER IN MOORHEAD, MINNESOTA

JUST PAST MIDNIGHT, ON SATURDAY, JULY 28, 2007

Lawrence Welk didn't do drugs. At least non-prescriptive. But that doesn't mean they don't show up in his book.

One night in Selby, South Dakota, according to *Wunnerful, Wunnerful*, a silent man in a broad-brimmed hat watched the band, leaning against a post in the back edge of the audience. In the evocative prose distinguishing McGeehan from ghostwriting celebrity hacks, she says this man possessed an "actor's face" and "a large nose."

"Good evening, sir. My name is George T. Kelly! I've enjoyed your little novelty orchestra so much and may I say that you are the finest young accordionist it has ever been my pleasure to hear . . ."

Always with the squeezebox compliments.

The next morning, over pie and the world's most delightful coffee (Kelly's opinion, not Welk's), they agreed Welk would go on the road with Kelly, splitting profits 50-50.[1] It's the beginning of what Welk refers to as "his most happy days" singing, dancing, playing accordion as a member of the Peerless Entertainers vaudeville troupe. It also marks a period when Welk appears on stage as a trampy stereotype called "the Spaniard" during a murder-mystery sketch and "Ole the Swede/Norwegian" depending on local Scandinavian alliances, from about North Dakota to Texas.

Anyway, Lawrence learned tons.

---

1. On our journey to Strasburg, Carrie and I also found Selby, South Dakota, where Welk and Kelly enjoy their breakfast, but I found no café and certainly no hotel.

Like how to look the part.

"I bought clothes like his (Kelly's)—flashy outfits with striped vests—and I learned how to tuck my right hand casually into the watch pocket of the vest as he always did, which made me feel very sophisticated."

And the proper ratio for performers to audience members.

"I'm sorry, madam," Kelly tells the audience of one lady in Enid, Oklahoma, "We make it a rule that there must be more people in the audience than in the cast."

And, lastly, how to lie.

"What kind of pie is this!?!" Lawrence barks at a waitress.

After the show, George, who had smiled and tipped the waitress extravagantly, wakes up Lawrence in the car. "Wherever you go you leave an impression," George says, "Now it's up to you whether you leave a good one or a bad one."

But that summer, as George went back north, Lawrence drove a band across Texas panhandle country and received a real education.

It was during the wild oil days. When pistol play broke out, the maestro dove behind the piano, his accordion squeezing to a stop. One night his saxophonist—who grinned at a cowboy's comely wife—got his abdomen slashed by a knife and needed stitches.

On another night, Lawrence encountered the musician's chemical nemesis.

During breaks, he writes, the hired musicians kept disappearing out behind the dance hall during their scheduled breaks and returned "glassy-eyed."

Marijuana, he says.

"Even after they explained it," Welk admits, he still sat boggled.

―――――――――

It wasn't that I expected not to encounter drugs on tour. When Donny smoked during rehearsals in our old practice space, a rented garage in downtown Sioux Falls, he just threw open the door. Poncho, in a pinch, had sold from the back of a sub shop. But so far, on tour, we'd held them at bay.

Even on this night, we seemingly laughed the guy off.

I figured our north country street pharmacist had forgotten about us by the time we left the parking lot in the *Bly*. We rolled over a northbound Red River, past a closed Hornbacher's grocery store, a wan glow warming the plate-glass windows, and pulled up to a shopworn rambler of a house covered by two bushy conifers.

A woman, frazzled, met us on the stoop, saying they need fifteen minutes. So we made a 3 a.m. Taco Bell trip, and when we returned, a guy none of us knew stood in the driveway.

"Why don't you take your brother inside," Donny whispered.

So I grabbed our sleeping bags and trudged into the stranger's house.

Language is what still bothers me about the music scene. When the words made sense, when there was calibration, things were good. But when the words sagged or misdirected, chaos ensued.

My brother and I unrolled our sleeping bags on a sectional in the house. A ceiling fan rotated above us, as my brother collapsed into the couch.

More than anyone, the kid loved music. That's the only reason Leo was here. He'd written music since the eighth grade. He had sent money to Japan for records. But now loving music meant sleeping on a stranger's couch with some kind of shady deal outside. So I tried cheering him up.

"You ever realize that 'Barbara Ann' is only two minutes long?"

Leo stretched his arms over his head, his long hair splayed over the pillow.

"What's the point?" he sighed.[2]

I spotted my white socks dangling off the couch, glowing in the dark.

"Like, that song has as much cultural power as the *Mona Lisa* or *Moby Dick*," I protested, "except it's two minutes long. Two minutes to change the world!"

But Leo balked. He was too tired to be diverted into trivia.

"Goodnight, man. I'm not in the mood."

---

2. The eccentricities of Brian Wilson and the Beach Boys, in general, were a consistent theme of humor for us.

The green clock on the wall blinked. The ceiling fan spun. And I surrendered to sleep.

About thirty-five seconds later, the screen door swung open, cracking the frame. The voice curled around the fridge.

"All I'm saying is be cool, man."

"But you made me wait!"

Boots cluttered onto the kitchen floor.

I had never been around a drug deal—let alone one invoking Stephen Sondheim lyrics—so I wasn't sure how nervous to be.

"And you go to Taco Bell?"

Then, the stranger yelled.

"Give me twenty bucks!"

"Listen, you dropped it, man!"

The screen door flew open. Poncho picked himself off the fridge. When I looked up, Donny had his arms around the guy's shoulders.

"Get Leo outta here!" Monster yelled.

Huh? I thought. *Don't be melodramatic.*

He yelled again.

"Get your brother out of here!"

Without debate, I turned to the couch.

"Come on, dude," I said.

As some silverware spilled onto the floor, frantically, I led my brother to the bathroom.

"Just a minute."

And I closed the plywood door.

"Are you serious?"

But his voice was muffled.

[ARE YOU SERIOUS]

When I heard the *crack* of the screen door twice, rapid boots pounded back over wooden steps. From the kitchen window, I watched the melee's demise in the drive.

"Someone called me about a *trip!*" yelled the stranger, now revving his car.

My stomach sank. This was all a bad pun, a homonymic miscue.

"They meant a trip to Taco Bell!" Donny yelled, sticking up for us.

The stranger's faced wrenched up into almost saint-like pity. Then he slammed his car door.

Moments later, his tires squealed and shot him erratically down the street like a pinball under the heavy, late-summer foliage.

It all became too real. Trembling in the kitchen, I wished I could go back and dissuade that man of any confusion on the word "trip," or maybe never even played at the Nestor at all.

The door *creaked* open.

Strolling out of the bathroom, my kid brother fell back face-first into the sofa. When he rolled over, his neon Hoover Dam T-shirt glowed in the darkness.

<hr />

Wearing bright colors is a powerful burden. You can see it on *The Lawrence Welk Show*. In the early 1960s, when they splendidly joined technicolor, no one looks reduced beneath costumes. Pianist JoAnn Castle with the ocean spray beehive moves her fast fingers on the honky-tonk, while Guy Hovis reclines in a muskmelon ranch jacket lonesome howling:

I ain't a gonna marry in the fall.
I ain't a gonna marry in the spring.

The smiles match the hydrangea dresses. The bright eyes complement the Neapolitan ice cream tuxedos and shiny trombones. The visuals are the music.

On the morning that I picked up the book, depressed as I was, that's what I felt holding that book, staring at the glossy photographs on Grandma's linoleum kitchen floor: color. It lifted us from the prairie. His band, the Honolulu Fruit Gum Orchestra, glowed like a green Jolly Rancher, pure, juicy fruit, in a field wracked by black blizzards. And the joy of creation glittered in my own sullen mind.

I ain't a gonna marry in the fall.
I ain't a gonna marry in the spring.

"You okay, Leo?" I asked, alarmed.

He murmured something inaudible.

I had failed to steer us from danger. I had been silent, complicit. Shame swelled inside me; some Catholic guilt, or motherly echo, stirred me. This wasn't what Collette or Heather or my mother, Rita, or my grandmothers, Delores or Virginia, would expect of me. This wasn't what I expected of me.

After pacing the yellow linoleum in the kitchen, with the guys walking silently up to the screen door, I knew to protect Leo.

My bandmates leaned haunches against countertops. Standing in the kitchen, I cleared my throat.

"Um," I said, tentatively, "I have something to say."

Everyone looked up, and I momentarily froze.

The gentle buzz of the cicadas outside *see-see-see-saawed*.

The ceiling fan oscillated.

"We're waiting, Chris," Monster said, peering out the window.

"It's not a rule," I stammered, gaining strength. "But, well, uh, no more acid deals on tour."

It was a cautious line in the sand to draw. But if I didn't draw it, I feared what else might drive down the street.

"Especially with my brother," I added.

Then, I waited for their retaliation.

I've thought long and hard about what the right thing to do in this moment was. Welk never reprimands his band, at least down in the Texas Panhandle. But Welk also didn't look after his little brother. He also didn't have command of the English language. He hadn't graduated college.

My ultimatum may have been the puniest thing ever uttered by a musician in the history of tours. But I couldn't take it back now.

Bobby picked up the Foreman grill, placed it back on the counter, and to my relief, he agreed.

"Chris is right," he said. "That was out of control."

Donny, too, leaned against the kitchen island, nodding his head.

"I'll smoke a little weed, but no more acid. Not with your brother around."

"That's cool," Poncho said. "We were talking Radiohead's *The Bends* and the next thing I know—*wammo,* up against the fridge."

"Not to spoil the mood, but didn't that guy say he was coming back?" asked Monster.

Apparently, while I had been tending to Leo in the bathroom, the dealer had threatened, prior to climbing into his car, to "take out on the house" everything he felt we owed him.

Donny busily scratched out a note to the homeowners passed out in the basement: "Sorry, your friend tried to kill us."

"Alright, let's get out of here."

The Brickhouse Boys packaged our sleeping bags, hustled out to the van (the house's owners were passed out and heard nothing), and piled into the *Bly,* roaring off down the block.

I've tried to imagine whether Welk would've approved of my outburst, if he would've accepted my ground-rules, and I think, at least in that moment, he would've had sympathy with me. I had tried to keep our band focused, business-like.

Within minutes of driving around, we spotted an elementary school playground and unrolled sleeping bags on the equipment—slides and tunnels—and leaned back against a cool slide.

And we also evaded danger.

"Night, losers!" Bobby said.

"Keep an eye out for that dude!"

"Whatever! Goodnight!"

Under the stars, I watched for any circling IROC, but my brother, whose mood had improved, yelled out to Poncho.

"Did you know that Mike Love wrote the melody line on Brian Wilson's 'Good Vibrations?'"

"Goodnight, Leo . . ." Poncho yelled. "And I knew that."

"I'm picking up 'good vibrations!' She's giving me exultations!"

"It's *excitations,* Leo!" Poncho yelled.

"What's that? Are you serious? What are *excitations?*"

"It's a Mike Love lyric, that's what that is," called Bobby.

The lyric lifted into the violet morning. From the black and quieted homes surrounding us like sleepy little snails, men and women were likely getting up early for work, turning on coffee pots, brushing teeth, and maybe, if they listened closely, they could've heard the distant sound like wind chimes coming from somewhere near the playground of grown men laughing.

CHAPTER 13

LAWRENCE WELK VILLAGE IN ESCONDIDO, CALIFORNIA

FRIDAY, MARCH 29, 2019

A few years ago, Leo, Carrie, and I drove in a rental car from San Diego to Los Angeles and stopped off on the business end of the I-5 to Lawrence Welk's resort in Escondido. You can't miss it: a golf course nestled under a cacti-baked mountain with a restaurant and an air-conditioned theater that was hosting "Menopause: The Musical" that week.

Our waitress was flabbergasted by our repeated questions for trivia and dispatches. Finally, either frustrated or perhaps learning what we—against the projection of our youth—were actually after, the waitress brayed, "Oh, we've got some nostalgia you can look at in the old theater."

She said "nostalgia" like a bandana-wearing woman who keeps a boa constrictor in her mini-van at the flea market might say "trinkets" or "flare."

"People love looking at the nostalgia," she said, waving her hands, referring to the generations before who no longer drank our same air. "Yeah, that's where you'll find that, if it's what you're looking for."

We ordered our meals. Nothing Welk-related. A burger. A salad. I got some room-temperature, watery noodles. The music in the background carried an internet radio station stuck on 1970s soft rock like Looking Glass and Nanci Griffith.

"Wonder when they stopped trying to court the Welk audience," I said, trying to outrun any anticlimactic dread.

"Probably around the same time the guy's audience all got wheeled into the nursing home," said my brother.

Lawrence Welk migrated west with the country. Sometimes, when I'm looking for Welk back in the Dakotas, I remember he's no longer there. He moved to California in the early 1950s after a career in the east and took with him the rarified bliss of frenzied, not foul Saturday nights.

Although he represented the Upper Midwest's most visible contribution to American popular culture, he wasn't the only one. There was the late-night host, Johnny Carson, from Norfolk, Nebraska. Flamboyant pianist Liberace grew up in a Milwaukee suburb. This coastal matriculation—at least, then—felt deserved, normal, ordinary.

Of course, you only need to drive down Wilshire Avenue and see the dilapidated Beverly Wilshire Hotel and scraps of turquoise paint on chipped buildings to realize he's not in California, either.

I ordered a gin and tonic and my brother, a beer. Carrie, restless, walked over to a couple dining near us—the man wore a Mount Rushmore baseball cap—and point-blank asked if they liked Welk.

The woman pursed her lips and shook her head.

"Some people think his music is elevator music."

The man, her husband, curtly nodded.

"But it's not bad," he said. "He's got some good stuff."

"Do you come here often?" Carrie asked.

"The place used to be a lot nicer," the man said, bluntly.

His hands grasped his bony elbows, arms folded underneath the table. The air conditioning may've been a degree or two too cold.

"Nicer?" Carrie asked.

"It used-ta-have nicer furnishings."

I looked back over my shoulder to my brother, to see if he was catching any of this, but he just stared at his beer.

Carrie and I had flown out to see him and his new band play in San Diego. But the night before our flight, he'd sent a strange text message.

"There's been an accident."

It had been late on the east coast. Mom was on the text, so I figured she would handle any emergency. When I got into LAX, under those familiar green and yellow palm trees sticking up behind the rental cars, I called Leo.

"They're all dead," he said.

I gasped.

For two weeks, his band had toured the West opening up for a British indie duo called Her's. A Minneapolis guy we knew drove and sold merch for Her's.

But on Tuesday night after playing in Phoenix, a drunk driver barreled the wrong way down a desert interstate and struck the band's van. By the time firefighters arrived, no one knew who they were.

No one got word out.

A night later, in Santa Monica, when my brother's band plugged in guitars and set up for soundcheck, Her's didn't walk through the doorway. People were curious after thirty minutes. After forty-five minutes, anxious. After an hour, panicked.

"Don't be crazy," Leo said. "They're going to walk in here any moment."

But they didn't. Frantic internet searching began. After reading a state patrol report with an accompanying video of their touring van charred, the phone calls started.

"Just gone," Leo told me over the phone, as I stood near the Ubers.

"In a blink."

I asked him if he would still come to San Diego with us.

"Better than sticking around here."

We drove downtown to LA, picked him up, and headed to San Diego. We walked the beach, watched the sunset, hoping to see the green pulsation of energy that supposedly explodes right at the setting sun.

"Just like in science, man," Leo said, as we walked up the sand hill. "Energy is neither created nor destroyed."

A Coast Guard truck quietly zipped down the hill to a base. That night, we got back in our rental and headed for dinner and beers, laughing at all the scooters twirling around downtown San Diego. Then we all slept in the same bed, owing to our tiny AirBnB. It felt like being on tour again.

There is a timelessness that musicians inhabit. A track they're running separate from our own, and I can still remember the details— the Doritos wedged under the van's windshield, the soundchecks, the late nights.

While visiting La Crosse, Wisconsin, a few years after our tour, I ran into a band that we had played with in Fargo. I was teaching English at a college on the bluffs upriver in Winona, Minnesota. They were still touring, and I thought about time travel, like, what if I simply stayed playing and then emerged—twenty-seven and thin and vegan, hard and much better at piano—and saw a guy grading papers and drinking an IPA with a soft belly in the corner. Would I regret not being him?

In the morning, Carrie and I went on a run, passing the small, barking dogs behind chain link fences in our neighborhood of San Diego, stopping for coffee at an open-air bar with an alligator skeleton above the barista's head, and after we ran back, Leo had roused.

Clicking through my phone, I found an article on *USA Today* that carried the story of the band's tragic accident in the desert.

Like I had in Moorhead some twelve years earlier, I tried cheering Leo up, noting their music would now be heard by more people than ever before.

But he swatted that away.

"They wouldn't care about that," he said. "They weren't those type of guys. They just loved what they were doing."

In Welk's hard days on the road as a young musician, even in the leanest times, when his pocketbook could fold in on itself from lack of funds and he would drive all night to avoid paying for a hotel room for the band, even then, that North Dakota troubadour had a master plan, a purpose. But that's the problem with memoirs. Real life doesn't have plot points.

When I awoke back in late July 2007, perched on a quickly heating slide on Saturday morning in the middle of a playground outside an elementary school in Moorhead the morning after our encounter with a drug dealer, I just slid down and walked to the McDonald's. The thirty minutes I spent reading the *Fargo Forum's* softball box scores and eating a hash brown served no purpose, save it would be among my most solitary moments on tour. No one around. No sound guys yelling at me. No drug dealer. The tiny freedom of a greasy egg McMuffin exhilarated. I felt normal. Normal was good.

In Escondido, our server brought us the food, and we dug in. I'd ordered my gin and tonic in honor of when Welk—at the William Penn Hotel in Pittsburgh, in trying to impress a richer, more refined crowd—broke his no-alcohol rule and ordered a gin and tonic and, mistaking the swizzle stick for a straw, proceeded to dump the entire drink on his lap.

"Have you seen the statue of the man?" our waitress asked, when she returned with a refill of water.

"That's kind of nostalgia-like."

The theater was closed, but we peered in at the dark lobby and saw a large wall print of Welk and his baton, smiling back at us. Then we walked over to the statue, hiding amongst some flowers.

"It's certainly not life-sized," I told them, as it came up to my shoulders.

Welk was about six foot three. His life-sized cardboard cutout (in a white velour suit) appears in the homestead back in Strasburg.

"Let's take a photograph, anyway," Carrie said.

We did. We then got into a car and were preparing to drive away when we spotted a rock-strewn fountain welcoming people off the side of the road. Two small children climbed the rocks behind us.

"We're looking for a geocache," the older girl said.

"Fun!" Carrie said.

"Have you ever heard of Lawrence Welk?" I asked.

The girl looked up at me with a funny expression.

"Yeah," she said. "He's got that statue, right?"

***

The Brickhouse Boys returned Saturday night to the Nestor. We didn't pound out our set like Friday, but we played competently, opening up for some touring band from Athens, Georgia, and around 2 a.m., we boarded the *Bly* and headed to my family's cabin in northern Minnesota. The guys mostly slept, but I drove. Donny sat up front.

"Be alert," he said. "This is when all the drunks are out."

Donny and I had taken English classes together, but in all our time together I still had no idea what he planned for a career after school.

"What would you do if your bands don't work out?" I asked.

The motor rumbled beneath us. He lit a cigarette, sounds of wind whistling through the crack in the window.

"Probably move to New York, walk dogs, be a session drummer on Broadway."

Lines already grooved into Donny's forehead at twenty-six. He had an inexhaustible approach to music. As the conversation ebbed, we traded ear buds back and forth playing songs out of our iPods.

"Listen to this," he said.

I had never heard Elliott Smith's "Waltz #2."

"It sounds like a rusty swing set," I said.

"Nice," he said.

Telephone wires drooped elliptically from one pine pole to the next along the highway. Donny practiced paradiddles on the steering column with his thumbs.

"Here," I said, calling up "American in Paris."

My parents fed me a heavy diet of music from classical public radio as a child. Some of my earliest memories were in our home in Kiester, Minnesota, just before bed, Mom slipping one of Dad's big T-shirts around me, the black-and-yellow Yankton College number, and then playing Modest Mussorgsky's "Night on Bald Mountain" on the record player, as I flew around the cushy couch and carpeted living room, tiring myself out.

I fast-forwarded to the trumpet's signature wail.

"Whenever I hear this," I said, "I see a Parisian streetscape at night, and a man in a trench-coat just waving and walking into the dark. It's not jingoistic, but it makes you feel good to be an American, right?"

The line connecting the headphones bobbed between us. In the ditch, the eyes of a deer glowed red by the flash of headlights, as the road curved tightly around a pine grove. Donny lifted his black All-Stars onto the dashboard as the broadcast from the BBC lulled like a boat out to static waters.

"You ever think of writing about music instead of making it?"

The van swallowed up yellow-striped lines, plunging into a dark forest. Wind swept into the van's interior and then out the vented windows in back, rustling Doritos bags, our sleeping bandmates' hair.

"Like reviews?" I asked.

"Don't get me wrong, I love your songwriting, but maybe other stuff, too. You seem to have a different way of talking about it."

No one had told me that before.

I tightened my grip self-consciously on the steering wheel.

"Thanks, but words are never as good as sounds, you know," I said. "Other than onomatopoeia, what is there?"

Soon we got lost. I missed a turn in the rain. We went an hour or more out of the way. But Donny didn't say anything. If someone would've lifted the *Bly's* roof and peeked in, they would've just called this leisure. Going camping with friends. At around 6 a.m., we arrived on the pine-tree shores of Little Mantrap Lake in northern Minnesota. As sun glinted through the Pixar-created forest, the puffy-faced Brickhouse Boys shuffled noiselessly into the small wooden cabin, my aunt, uncle, and cousin sleeping in the bedrooms, and we fell asleep while a loon announced in soft *coo-COOS* the arrival of morning.

CHAPTER 14

THE RED SEA BAR IN MINNEAPOLIS, MINNESOTA

In my family's cabin, photos document the inhabitants, from white-bearded men in black and white hoisting lines of walleye to babies in yellow, plastic wash tubs. My dad's dad is everywhere in those photos: a portly, happy Bohemian woodsman with his elfin eyes squished by a fishing cap, dipping his twinkle toes into the bubbling headwaters of the Mississippi River or marching with his Nebraska band.

One photo is missing, though: a wood-paneled backdrop with four men in glasses, squeaky red vests, and white dress shirts, emblazoned with the words "Barn Dancing Polka Style."

This was Grandpa's vinyl LP.

At his funeral in 2009, at St. Wenceslaus Catholic Church in Verdigre, my family, as somber as ivory faces of the saints, moved heavily into the final verse of "How Great Thou Art" when the organ upstairs stopped playing.

Everyone looked up, confused.

The staid priest's mouth dropped open.

Then they started back in—my uncle on trumpet, playing the lilting barroom melody to the "Pennsylvania Polka."

To that happy *oom-pa-pa* we waltzed Grandpa's ashes out to the hearse.

My grandfather's memoir is only ten pages, and he misspells "band" as "bard," but he recalls one of those nights Welk came to town.

Maybe "bard" was correct.

Piles of people crammed into the Hill Top Pavilion, normally a burger joint or gymnasium with balance rings, and Leo Kotrus took a long, wooden pole off the wall with a small, silver hook to unlatch a chain, swinging open the wooden eyelashes to a mighty *smack*, echoing over the river valley.

"Got a band coming tonight! You maybe heard him on WNAX!"

Cars streamed in with the pharmacist, teachers, postman, cheekbones red as grilled tomatoes; cowhands talked to the new librarian, who adjusted her wireless frames, her green eyes intently studying his broad forehead, his stammer.

Under the bridge, a chubby Bohemian boy one week off of feeding ginger snaps to Grizzlies in Yellowstone hung from the balance beams beneath, collecting strewn bottle tops.

But at 8 p.m., the bard wasn't there.

Impatient, mercenaries went up the hill. It had rained. The alpine roads easily washed out. Sure enough, they found him.

When Lawrence decided to leave the "most exciting city" he had ever seen, he wanted to go south.[1] To Dixieland music, to New Orleans. So, after an "unseasonal blizzard blanketed the city with several feet," the young maestro gathered his three bandmates into the car.

But the death-defying winter travel—no heater, snow piled high on the shoulder—encumbered the travelers, and by 3 a.m, they landed in the Collins Hotel in Yankton, asleep before the door closed.

They would stay for roughly a decade.

---

1. Which, if you're just joining us, is known more colloquially in this text as Bismarck, North Dakota.

Like Nashville's WSM ("We Shield Millions") opened to sell life insurance and carried *The Grand Ole Opry* as an afterthought, Yankton's WNAX Radio Station started in 1922 to market Gurney Seed and Nursery, which sold invasive flowering species across the country.

During summers in the 1970s, my dad worked at this mail-order seed company, driving east along the river bottoms to propagate rose bushes.

"Gurney's was a good summer gig," Dad said. "They even made us watch a company history video."

In one of those videos grinned Chan Gurney, grandson to the company CEO and proprietor of WNAX, when a young North Dakotan maestro who struggled with English pronunciation walked into his offices a day after a big blizzard threatening to play "Mexicali Rose."

If someone ever points out the general unfairness of America, one might look no further than the fact that Lawrence Welk and not, say, Tito Puente, possessed a longstanding weekly primetime dance show on television.

In the 1980s, Puente even appeared on *Sesame Street*. He's clicking drum sticks over trash cans on a New York street, when Oscar the Grouch interrupts him.

"Who are you and whadya doing here?" asks the green Muppet from a trash can.

"I was about to start my band and play a number"

"Oh yeah, well my name is Oscar the Grouch."

A back and forth ensues, during which Puente starts up his band, and Oscar's minions bob and swing over to Puente's drums. You can't tell me that wouldn't have sold Dodge Darts.

But somehow America got stuck with Welk.

It could've been worse, certainly. Welk was a lifelong troubadour. A road-show warrior. And among his cowboy crooners, blonde pianists, and Norwegian accordionists, Welk's cast reflected a smattering of American diversity, at least more than most midcentury sitcoms.

While *The Lawrence Welk Show* was not exactly the S.S. *Pequod*, in 1964 the maestro hired tap-dancer Arthur Duncan, who became one of the first Black performers on a TV variety show. And in the 1970s, he also started regularly featuring singer Anacani (Maria Conseulo Castillo-López y Cantor-Montoya), who worked as a hostess at his restaurant in Escondido and had emigrated with her family as a child to the United States from her home along the Sea of Cortez in Mexico.

Still, a white man with an accordion waltzing into the living rooms of 1950s Alpena and Peoria was probably—network producers figured—going to sell more Geritol than Duke Ellington or Tito Puente.

And if you doubt Welk's success derived from his palatability as a vehicle for home-good products, I would just point to the vinyl records my father kept on our bookshelf: Louis Armstrong, Benny Goodman, Count Basie.

But no Welk.

Why? Because my father didn't want to just hear good music. He wanted the best. And that didn't include the Polka Elvis.

Still, Welk had a clever mind and a working-man's heart, honed in the Midwest.

WNAX's signal could be heard from Fargo down to Omaha, and Welk impressed Gurney, who signed the orchestra to a week's contract. Then a month, three months; finally, he was a regular.

Every morning at 6 a.m. and afternoon at 2 p.m., according to a velour commemorative book bearing old WNAX schedules I once held in Lu Ella's living room, Lawrence Welk and His Novelty Orchestra danced into your kitchen, your barn, your porch.

And on weekends, they'd gallivant out to the country towns.

When the Verdigre boys drove up into the bluffs over the Missouri River, they spotted an orchestra stranded, with a tall man in a white suit, jacket off, pushing on a tire, the ring glittering on his pinky finger.

"*Vitame vas!*" cried Welk.

The crowd doubled, Grandpa wrote, roaring as yellow headlights came down the hill. When the car door burst open, the man in the dazzling white suit flew out, squeezing his twinkling accordion like one inelegantly manages a frantic cat out of a tree, whirling into the pavilion, sucker punching the night.

That Sunday, the Brickhouse Boys swam in the lake, grilled hot-dogs, and leisurely reclined in the Adirondack chairs as humming-birds *flit-flit-flitted* from pine to pine, as Uncle Tom, Aunt Kathy, and Cousin Ellie talked music.

"It's a grind, isn't it?" asked Uncle Tom.

Tom, like my dad, had played in bands back in Nebraska, South Dakota, and Minnesota. He'd known a little of that life but settled into playing weekends over in Marshall, a little college town on the prairie where someone could always sleep in their own bed. My aunt sighed, spreading jelly with a knife onto some toast.

"You know, Grandpa and Grandma would be proud to see you using your musical talent," Kathy said. "But it's a grind."

When the sun peaked highest above the lake, the Brickhouse Boys climbed back into the *Bly* and blew out of Northern Minne-sota toward Minneapolis and the Red Sea Bar. Around St. Cloud, my phone buzzed again with a text message. I figured it was Collette only catching me up on new trivia. But it was a new number.

"Christopher. What time do you go on?"

I had forgotten to text her back.

"Who's that?" Monster asked, grabbing my phone.

For nearly a week, Josie, the chain pharmacy heiress, and I had exchanged Facebook messages about books, puns, and the like. But I hadn't told the guys.

"What's going on?" Bobby asked, looking around.

"Josie's texting Chris back here," said Monster.

"Josie?" asked Donny, his eyes flashing into the rearview mirror.

"You know she dated Angus," Bobby remarked.

Minutes after the show had started, Donny slammed the *Bly*, increasingly papered-over in Subway wrappers, onto the hot, pul-verized, concrete parking lot behind The Red Sea Bar. A dumpster emitted a bouquet of spoiled fruit from its rotten belly. The opening act, a buck-toothed, red-haired man on guitar and his sister on drums in a punk duo, wailed on stage as we loaded in.

The Brickhouse Boys took the stage to maybe ten people.

But we had gotten decent. Maybe even good.

Each tune had edges, sharp corners, and midway through, I saw her walk into the bar.

Welk says he loved Fern because she reminded him of women who never came to his shows. He wanted someone to be a harbor while he spun far out to sea, and I resonated with this instinctive search for ballast.

Shadows covered her face, but I recognized her Jackie Onassis hair, and on stage, feeling like her eyes were on me, I maybe rocked back and forth theatrically to gain her attention. I maybe vainly threw my long hair like a lion's mane. After we finished, I climbed off stage, and Josie bounded right up.

"That was fantastic!" she said. "I mean I heard your guys' recordings," she plugged her nose. "But your live show has gotten so good."

I blushed. Her dark hair was pulled back now, tidily, so I could see a single stripe of green in her black hair.

Bobby, in a white V-neck T-shirt nearly sopping wet from sweat, clicked over in his dress shoes.

"What brings you out, Josie?" his legs dangled off-stage. "Angus didn't tell me anything."

She bowed, extravagantly, and spoke in a British accent.

"I don't know, sire. You should ask him."

She turned back to me and handed me a brown paper package.

"This is for you, as promised."

I tore off the top, and staring back at me was Ignatius J. Reilly of *Confederacy of Dunces*.

"It's about a hot dog vendor," Josie said. "The book. I thought you'd like it given what you told me about that jam band."[2]

"Oh, right," I grinned. "I'd love to read this so we could talk, but . . ."

"You guys need a place to stay?"

"What happens on tour stays on tour" wasn't any life motto, but when the band split that night, with my brother, Bobby, and Monster staying with friends near Dinkytown, Poncho, Donny, and I followed Josie's speedy, blue jeep into Lowry Hill, and I cupped a lark of hope.

We parked the gangrenous *Bly* underneath a bushy shade tree and tiptoed past the fancy townhomes.

"I'm going to sleep out in the van," Poncho said. "Just to protect the stuff."

We waved him off, and Josie led us up the stairs. She had a surprisingly big apartment with a butcher block island and cast-iron skillets hanging from the ceiling. She grabbed a feast of real food—cheese, crackers, fruit, and a bottle of wine—and led us out to a three-season porch overlooking a lush garden. Like filthy, denim-clad lemurs, we eased onto the cushioned wicker furniture.

"Christopher," Josie said. "I've got to add to your 'This Day in History' collection. There was this rodeo champion, a real cowboy, named Casey Tibbs."

"Never heard of this man," Donny said.

"He won like nine times," I said, recounting my magazine research. "But when he went to Hollywood, a film director told him he was too short to play a cowboy in a movie."

"How's that for a metaphor?" Josie remarked.

The night spun in concentric circles of the Dresden Dolls and Sam Cooke and purple meniscus lines. Around 4 a.m., Donny got up and said he needed to get some sleep, leaving just Josie and me above the garden.

A mourning dove *coo-coo'd.*

"Hey, you want to see my books?" she asked.

---

2. I had told her back in Pierre about our interaction with Governor's Suite, noting I felt more camaraderie with hot dog vendors than I did with jam bands.

We walked down a dark hallway, hitching a left into a room dreamily lit by the moonlight.

"I've read this," I said, grabbing Jerzy Kosinski's *Steps*.

"A professor assigned it to us in college," she said. "Supposed to help with our pacing."

"Hmmmm."

I creaked open the thin, greyish book. The orderly text spilled into the light. I flipped each page, knowing what story I wanted to read.

"Ahem," I said, clearing my throat. "*I won a prize in a photographic contest sponsored by a society for the old and infirm . . .*"

"Are you going to read this to me?"

"*She was a secretive person . . . All she said was that her life was her own.*"

"This is the climax I bet," Josie said.

Her hair pulled back at her ears, so now her face was shaped like a heart. She leaned close to me as I read.

"*She was lying naked on the bed, half covered by the furry body of a creature with a human head, pawlike hands, and the short, barrel-chested trunk of an ape.*"

"What?" Josie laughed. "What scandalous thing . . ."

"It's so random!" I said. "But, kind of spectacular, too, no?"

The sun warmed the room, nearing 5 a.m. now. Her lips pressed into mine. We fell onto the bed. It's hard kissing after hours of drinking wine because your head is a purple grape ready to burst. The cool white sheets flared out beneath us, my head buzzing with darkness, and the book may have suspended in mid-air or fell onto the floor, I'm unsure.

Around noon, I woke up wearing her sweatpants, cut off midway at my calves, with a splitting headache and *Confederacy of Dunces* just below my hand on the wooden floor.

A young Lawrence Welk poses with his accordion in in this 1942 photograph by Maurice Seymour. *North Dakota State University Libraries*

The Welk Homestead, photographed here in summer 2016, was built in 1899 and is now a historic site open to visitors. *Author photograph*

The Gurney Seed building became the home of the WNAX radio station in Yankton, South Dakota. Welk and his band made several live appearances on the station while it was housed in this building. *South Dakota State Historical Society*

Lawrence's parents, Ludwig and Christina, stand outside of their home in Strasburg, North Dakota, in 1934. *North Dakota State Library*

A bridge in Milltown, South Dakota, connected the mainland to an island that once housed a pavilion and dance hall where Welk frequently played. *Author photograph*

Welk smiles as he exits Rockefeller Plaza in New York in the late 1940s. *William P. Gottlieb Collection, Library of Congress*

The four Lennon Sisters—from left to right, Kathy, Diane, Peggy, and Janet—began appearing on the *Lawrence Welk Show* in 1955. *Stephen Taksler Collection, Georgia State University Library*

A sign on the outskirts of Interior, South Dakota, boasts of notable moments from the town's history, which include hosting several performances by Welk's band. *Author photograph*

In this 1961 photograph, Lawrence Welk dances with Norma Zimmer, who served as a "Champagne Lady" on the *Lawrence Welk Show* for twenty years. *Stephen Taksler Collection, George State University Library*

The Corn Palace in Mitchell, pictured here in 1965, hosted two memorable performances by both Welk earlier in the decade. Just over forty years later, the Brickhouse Boys would perform outside of the venue. *South Dakota State Historical Society*

Welk donated money to build the municipal pool in Strasburg, North Dakota, which still operates today and bears his name. *Author photograph*

Edna Stoner (left), Lawrence Welk, Edna's niece, and an unidentified woman shared a meal together during one of Welk's tours through South Dakota. *Courtesy of the McGill Family*

(*left*) After an initial television run at the Aragon Ballroom in Venice, California, Welk's syndicated program relocated to the Hollywood Palladium on Sunset Strip, seen here in 2016. *Author photograph.* (*right*) Lawrence Welk was laid to rest in Culver City, California, following his death on May 17, 1992. *Author photograph*

The Brickhouse Boys performed at the Chesterfield in downtown Sioux City, Iowa, in 2007. *Dietr Van Poppen photograph*

The author (keyboard) and his brother Leo (bass) performed an outdoor show with the Brickhouse Boys at a birthday party in Brandon, South Dakota. The band's touring van can be seen in the background. *Mel Travis photograph*

This image shows the author performing with his band, the Golden Bubbles, in 2009, two years after the Brickhouse Boys broke up. *Dietr Van Poppen photograph*

During a visit to the Welk Homestead near Strasburg, North Dakota, in 2016, the author posed with a cardboard cutout of the famous musician.
Carrie Johnson photograph

In 2017, the author stood with the Lennon Sisters for a photograph before their performance at the Grand Falls Casino in Larchwood, Iowa. *Grand Falls Casino and Resort*

In 2018, on an assignment for the *Rapid City Journal*, the author interviewed a rancher on her pasture in Fall River County, in southwestern South Dakota. *Ryan Hermens photograph*

CHAPTER 15

7TH ST ENTRY IN DOWNTOWN MINNEAPOLIS, MINNESOTA

WEDNESDAY, AUGUST 1

Of course, Welk made mistakes.

There was that show in the late 1960s when Welk's Champagne Music Makers performed a mawkish, "Let's Make America What It Used to Be," threatening to take a broom to sweep up Harlem. There's also his maudlin, mustachioed George Cates-helmed version of "April in Paris," creeping along like a photographic negative of Count Basie's jauntier interpretation.

But these are purely aesthetic regrets. What's odder, to me, is his inability to express genuine humility throughout *Wunnerful, Wunnerful.*

Woe dots his career, such as when Welk's wife threatens to leave him when he won't return from California to help her raise the kids, or when he misses his parents' funeral, or when he throws out the Lennons. But Welk sidesteps drama.

Once, talking with his grandson on the phone at the pandemic's start, I ran past cherry trees and stopped in the bowels of the U.S. Department of Agriculture to get better reception.

"Well, you know why he got famous, right?"

A car with Minnesota plates curiously flew past.

"He was *obsessed.*"

Over those next few days, while the Brickhouse Boys rehearsed and recorded an album in the basement of some friends in St. Louis Park, a small guilt rose over my night with Josie. Our texting stopped, beyond an exchange or two on O'Toole, and I wondered if I had erred, getting distracted, indulging the road's harbor town.

But those feelings soon washed under other problems like a log submerged in a stream. The slightest frayed tensions emerged between Bobby and me. Outside a Fargo coffee shop, we fought over harmonies. On Tuesday, returning to the Red Sea, he scolded me for forgetting my power cable (again).

"There's nothing you can do," Poncho told me that night around a fire. "He'll be all into your group and then he'll get *carried* away to something else."

But on Wednesday morning, I awoke to word we'd scored a gig at First Avenue.

"It's not technically First Avenue," Poncho told us, over reheated White Castle. "It's called 7th St Entry. It's right next door to First Avenue."

"They got room for like a twenty-minute set is all," Monster added.

Even with the qualifications, our heads filled with aspirations. Anyone could walk into a show in downtown Minneapolis: Prince's old bandmates, critics from the *City Pages*.

Poncho emailed bloggers and music writers. Donny texted old friends. Even Leo, my bashful brother, got on MySpace and announced our show time. In the basement, I finished piano tracks.

"One, two, three," Noah, our sound man whose day job was recording Garrison Keillor's *A Prairie Home Companion*, called.

I raised my hands onto the piano.

"Okay . . ."

I played for a few bars, while the guys sang group chorus harmonies.

Then, the tape cut out.

"Hey!"

Noah's voice came plaintively over the cans.

"Bridge fell."

"What?" I asked, getting defensive. "I *wrote* the bridge."

"No," Noah, said, confused. "Bridge over the Mississippi."

The words reassembled like alphabet cereal swirling.

"It just fell in the river."

I felt discombobulated, almost *embarrassed* that the world was happening right along with us. That's the winnowing narrows of the musician, the smallest capacity for attention to life off tour.

Welk makes barely a blip of World War II in *Wunnerful, Wunnerful*. There's not much of an address, either, on the Civil Rights Movement or Vietnam. *It's only when events interrupted his schedule*, I observed bitterly, *that they matter*.

We flew into town on the interstate, hoping to beat traffic.

"Will they still even have it?" Donny asked.

"What side of the river are we on?" asked Monster.

Ambulances and emergency response vehicles with keening sirens flew past the *Bly*. Word came in one of the headliners from First Avenue, a rapper named Brother Ali, backed out of the show. He had known someone on the bridge. Parking on the street, we hustled in with our gear.

"You guys the openers?" the bespectacled sound-guy asked.

We nodded.

"Got enough time for like five songs. That's it."

In 1931, back in Yankton, Lawrence wed Fern in the Sioux City Cathedral. Lawrence's bandmates draped arms over the pews, still recovering from a late-night hootenany in Norfolk, Nebraska. After the spartan mass, the couple headed downtown to a grand hotel for a celebratory breakfast. The honeymoon plan was to play La Crosse, Milwaukee, and then reach Albany, where they would start a tour. Lawrence would even fit in a trip to Niagara Falls with Fern.

But before the toast, the *maître d'* escorted Lawrence to the front desk and handed him the phone.

"Mr. Welk, it's your booking agent."

His whole east coast tour was cancelled.

About twenty-five or so people stood against the back wall. We unloaded instruments, threw cases along the edges, and checked microphones.

"Shouldn't we wait?" I asked, scanning the crowd for VIPs vainly.

"Thanks for coming tonight," Bobby said, "Pretty weird to do a show."

And we kicked in.

Another classic rope-a-dope!

The Brick arrived tight and hard that night. Real, right angles on our songs. But the performance at 7th St Entry didn't lead to invitations from next door. Our six guys barely fit on the breadbox of a stage. I sat on my amp. Leo breathed over my neck. Donny dropped a tom. About a dozen skinny kids in tight denim folded arms over shoulders and leaned in back against black walls, staring dispassionately at us. A few people stood in line for beer. And it felt like we were missing a coalescing song, one that wrapped up all of our ideas into a singular, three-minute musical expression.

I pondered our reception like a Rubik's cube: *maybe they were there for another band? Maybe the mood suffered because they knew someone on the bridge? Maybe we just stunk?*

After four or five songs, the sound guy cut us off. We carried our equipment back through the narrow backstage to the heavy door and out into the downtown air, sirens bouncing off skyscrapers.

The Great Depression had caught up with Lawrence. No one could afford hotel ballroom dances when they lost their jobs. So with Fern, Lawrence drove that night to Wisconsin.

After the gig, the newlyweds went to the hotel where Lawrence signed the register, grabbed his luggage, and glided innocently off to the elevator, before the moralistic concierge took one look at the John Hancocks, scoffed, and called him back.

"Mr. Welk! I'm sorry sir, but we don't allow this sort of thing here."

Fern had not yet legally changed her name. Lawrence signed in to the hotel's guest book with "Lawrence Welk" and "Fern Renner."

Deeply chagrined, he erased "Renner" and put down "Mr. and Mrs. Welk."

Fern was practically in tears laughing, but the happy couple managed to make it upstairs, close the door, and put up the "do not disturb" sign.

But in the morning, Lawrence awoke to his new reality: his band had only one more show on the calendar: Milwaukee. There's no way they could return to the Dakotas now.

They headed to Chicago.

Somewhere along Hennepin Avenue in the *Bly*, I sat on the orange couch, the coils easing beneath me, my feet on the steel grate, as we turned left under a bridge, rolling past churches, an art museum, away from downtown.

"We need a new song," I said. "Something they can't ignore."

"Nah, we need an X factor," Donny said.

"Maybe dance moves?" said Monster. "Choreography?"

I couldn't listen. I felt numb, reprimanded by the crowd's indifference.

We rolled into Uptown, cell service returning, and our phones lit up with text messages, missed phone calls, voicemails. My phone buzzed multiple times. I looked down at a text message.

Chris. Give me a call. We need to talk.—ANGUS

I can't say I was any less guilty than Welk of a monomaniacal focus on the tour, clouding out the world's preoccupations.

Months earlier, President Bush had called for a twenty-thousand-troop "surge" of kids my age to go to Iraq. That May, a college student from Virginia Tech, his mental health deteriorating, calamitously took two semiautomatic pistols to campus and killed dozens of classmates. The United Nations that spring released its fourth climate change report, documenting unequivocally the ill effects of "anthropogenic greenhouse gas concentrations."

Now a bridge fell. America was crumbling, but here in early August, I still worried about getting my band famous, about getting over heartbreak, about slowing down this twister racing across the prairie.

When we reached a TGI Fridays in St. Louis Park, I stayed in the parking lot. It only took like a second for Angus to pick up. He had been drinking.

"What's up, Chris?"

"So you probably want to talk about Josie, right?"

He would take a more Socratic method.

"You called me. *What* Josie thing?!"

"Look, man, it was a late night. It was nothing, it just."

But Angus had anger in his voice.

"How would you like it if I had slept with Heather?"

I froze in the parking lot. A man in sandals and cargo shorts stumbled out.

"Listen, Angus," I said, more softly, trying to see straight. "I-I . . . I didn't, I mean . . ."

But I had no breath.

"You better hope we don't run into each other out in South Dakota when you're back from your tour."

And he hung up.

In the window, I watched my band, laughing, ordering appetizers, drinks being served, doing all the things a band on tour was supposed to do. But I could only stare at an anchor on the hoisted television, who talked about what was already known about "structural deficiencies," while a replay of the bridge—caught on a security camera—kept falling and falling and falling.

CHAPTER 16

OPEN MIC'S BAR, VERMILLION, SOUTH DAKOTA

THURSDAY, AUGUST 2, 2007

Musicians are famous for playing music, as distraction, as delusion, while calamity reigns.

A plucky brass band played "Nearer, My God, To Thee" while passengers boarded life rafts on the *Titanic* in the North Atlantic. Russian dissident Anastasia Vasilyeva played "Fur Elise" on a simple but in-tune upright while police raided her house in 2021. I've often, when losing hope, played piano by myself on a winter's night.

Music can be for itself, for rousing others' spirits, or for comfort. But I still think the fatal problem with our band compared to Welk's stood on a billboard just north of Sioux City, Iowa.

On the west side of the interstate, just outside a giant cattle feed lot, a billboard crawls out of the grass that says, "Support Your Local Ranchers. Eat Beef."

On that coming Friday night, as we drove toward Nebraska for a gig, my brother wryly pointed out its prophecy for us, too.

"That's the same argument musicians use. Listen to us because we're here."

Let me put it in economic terms.

Lawrence talks about playing three-day weddings as a kid. By the end, he had wrapped his hands in bandages. The straps cut him. Even in old age, he still claims scar tissue.

You might wonder why. But there was an incentive: money. The bride's father always paid him. In economic terms, he had a market.

But when I compared this to the Brickhouse Boys, I saw nothing. There was no demand, only supply. People weren't clamoring for Brickhouse. No sullen ballroom stared at an empty dance floor while we fought in the van. No bartender wondered, "Where's the Brick?" And we probably lost money on tour.

Our music was not needed.

In a poem by William Carlos Williams called "The Dance," he speaks about Pieter Brueghel the Elder's painting, *The Peasant Dance*:

> *In Brueghel's great picture, The Kermess,*
> *the dancers go round, they go round and*
> *around, the squeal and the blare and the*
> *tweedle of bagpipes, a bugle and fiddles*
> *tipping their bellies (round as the thick-*
> *sided glasses whose wash they impound)*
> *their hips and their bellies off balance*
> *to turn them. Kicking and rolling*
> *about the Fair Grounds, swinging their butts, those*
> *shanks must be sound to bear up under such*
> *rollicking measures, prance as they dance*
> *in Brueghel's great picture, The Kermess.*

The painting depicts revelers—kind of hideously—jigging, singing, tweedling, carousing on the Kermess. It's like a medieval *Lawrence Welk Show*.

In Welk's day, people needed live musicians. They couldn't get DJs or iPods. Weddings, funerals, bachelor parties, and Saturday night dances required musicians, otherwise there'd be no music. In *Wunnerful, Wunnerful's* Playskool Village universe, like a baker made bread, or a garbage man took out the trash, the musician entertained and delighted workers after a long day.

But when I look back on the Dakotas in 2007, on the Brickhouse Boys, I can see so many delayed-adolescence bands sleeping in elementary school parks or playing sparsely attended shows, while the world spun and collapsed and woke up again without them.

"Support Local Musicians. Listen to Local Bands."

This was the problem, the patronage model. We needed to reverse the expression.

"Support Good Music. Some of it is Local."

Although I doubted we could afford a billboard.

Lawrence writes in *Wunnerful, Wunnerful* that he spent a week in Chicago trying to honeymoon, walking the boardwalk, pointing at the Edgewater Hotel, a pink building straddling Lake Michigan, under a sliver moon.

"Someday I'm going to play there," he said, squeezing his wife's hand.

Fern doesn't say much in the book. Maybe she said, "Okay, honey." Or "yeah, right." Or "who did I marry?"

But we don't get any of that.

Lawrence escorts Fern to a Louis Armstrong show at a smoky bar, but when he looks down, Fern is confused.

"All at once I realized that what seemed like the greatest music to me was just a lot of noise to her. I realized also what kind of life I had put her into—one she would never have chosen for herself, but one she was determined to understand for my sake."

For my sake.

That this is all here, *for my sake.*

And in the morning, he drives back to South Dakota.

It was the same for us. We had another show offer at Mankato's What's Up Lounge, but our luck had run out. Bobby wanted to make his girlfriend Tina's graduation ceremony, so on Thursday morning, we drove the five hours back, stopping only for gas.

"Go get her!" Donny yelled, as the van pulled up next to the campus in Vermillion, only a week after we had left, primped with hydrangeas and low-hanging trees. I watched Bobby run across the grassy lawn of campus, with ivory Old Main shining, and I felt a tug of jealousy in my chest. *He landed on his feet.*

Donny sank the *Bly*, tired and EPA-flouting, into drive, and we moseyed past unpainted Victorian houses under deciduous trees that nearly touched each other in the late summer heat. When we finally pulled onto quiet Forest Avenue, I noticed the block had a new coat of pavement, but not my car.

"I forgot."

Donny spied me in the rearview mirror.

"They towed your car?"

I nodded.

"Why didn't someone call?"

"They did," I said, remorsefully.

On Sunday night, as I traipsed into Josie's, I had listened to a voicemail from my landlord, the mother who lived downstairs. She told me about the paving, about my car. But there was nothing I could do. I didn't even call her back.

It didn't need to be said: I had gotten carried away.

That next morning, after walking to the impound lot, I put the fee for $100 I didn't have on my credit card, flipped down my shades, and drove my Cavalier off into the river valley, a day on my own, with the windows down and the radio, blessedly, silent.

CHAPTER 17

SENIOR CITIZEN'S CENTER IN NORFOLK, NEBRASKA

SUNDAY, AUGUST 5, 2007

Earlier that summer, as I lounged on the porch swing, paging through *Wunnerful, Wunnerful,* I had been pulled by the central sacrilege of our protagonist: that Lawrence Welk, a Catholic boy, a Midwestern child, was going for fame.

Case in point: in one of the more bizarre but pleasing parts of the book, Lawrence lands in an Omaha priest's confessional asking the Father if his behavior, if being carried away with music, constituted a sin.

Weeks earlier, he crashed his van, injuring his band mates, and had woken up from nightmares (outside "Estherville, Ohio"). Lawrence tells the priest that sometimes when his band plays, "I do feel almost sinful at the tremendous pleasure it gives me."

Fortunately for Lawrence's eternal soul, the priest said in the long run, God is not antimusic, or even antipolka. Music is "a decent kind of pleasure that has brought happiness to men for hundreds of years."

I didn't feel like a sinner. But I felt like I had left the approved path. I fell short of not only my own expectations but also my family's idea of what I was supposed to be. And whatever dreams I revived in Vermillion—that night I ran through the rain after Bobby's text, some working musician who remained a good person—had clouded over after my venturing out on the road.

That Sunday afternoon, after more gigs in Sioux City and Lincoln, we drove to Norfolk, and I sat on the orange couch at the rear of the S.S. *Bly*. The cooler had a standing inch of water from melted ice and a couple of warm Mountain Dew cans rolling around. Poncho reread stories from a magazine he picked up at the bar. Monster slept in fetal position on the couch. Bobby stared out a window, the gusts tufting his hair like a general in those World War II movies cantering the aircraft carrier closer to Guam. And Donny smoked a cigarette, driving with his knees.

Next, perplexingly, we pulled into a senior citizens' center.

"What's happening, Poncho?" my brother asked. "What's going on here?"

"It's an emo festival," said Poncho.

"You've got to be kidding me!" cried my brother.

The scene burned like a bad, 1980s postapocalyptic movie. Kids with pink haircuts and ripped jeans spilled onto the green lawn. Punks leaned against the awning, smoking on the handicap-accessible rails. A few rusty vans parked dormant in the lot next to a suburban that shuttled members to the casino over in Sloan, Iowa. And I just knew this tasted fittingly like a good place for the Brickhouse Boys to bury itself.

When Lawrence—now in 1931, nearly thirty years old, on the road for nearly a decade—returns to Yankton, he writes, "Things picked up immediately." He fell into the old routine: WNAX by day, bandstands by night. But then he landed a two-night gig in Dallas, South Dakota.

Dallas, according to my dad, is a "dance hall at an intersection." His band gigged there in college. I once got lost on Highway 283 south of Pierre and landed at an intersection adjacent a dance hall: Dallas. Now the water tower and dance hall were boarded up. A lone donkey chewed on a can, monitoring the intersection.

Back then, when Lawrence arrived, he inspected the venue, ran his hands along the bleacher boards looking for splinters, and sprinkled sawdust on the floor. When he finished prepping, he walked past his bandmates meeting mysteriously in a pool hall.

"I felt vaguely uneasy, as I walked back to the hotel room."

The first night the band rounded up hundreds of dollars and returned to the hotel for sleep. In the morning, however, he had a mutiny on his hands.

I should've seen it coming, too. It's there in hindsight: Poncho sleeping every night in the van, Bobby's quiet chats with Donny, Monster posting to the Throwback's MySpace.

But Leo and I were oblivious.

On the grass eating food amongst the hacky-sack kickers, a friend from Vermillion walked past.

"Looking forward to seeing you guys open up for Thrice and Me-WithoutYou this fall," she called out.

The last few days had been dispiriting. In Sioux City, we had gone bar-to-bar trying to recruit fans so we could get some take-home pay at the venue. In Lincoln, Monster just sat with Poncho's overturned fedora asking for tips. I wanted off tour. But at her words, a curious spiral of ambition ran up my spine.

"Does she mean us?" I asked. "Like, we got an opening slot for a touring band?"

Opening for Thrice and MeWithoutYou—both established bands in the national post-hardcore/emo scene—might mean exposure to five hundred fans, maybe more. But Poncho's face whitened. Bobby looked down at the ground.

"I've been meaning to talk to you, Chris," Poncho said. "See, there's a big show this fall, but the promoters asked specifically for the Throwback."

"But the Throwback's dead," I scolded, my face hot as an oven-toasted biscuit. "Bobby told me. Right?"

Sure it made sense. The Throwback sounded like Foo Fighters, and Thrice was hardcore, emo. Kids would all be in black eyeliner.

I looked to my lead singer, remembering the night we'd talked on the phone, when he promised we would be the best band in the state.

But Bobby said nothing.

My eyes closed, defeated. We had never been anything but a fill-in for Bobby. He hadn't meant this as a serious group.

"But this would be huge for us!" I begged. "This is what we came on tour for!"

Bobby stood triumphantly on his two thin legs, his Levi's rolled over his Chuck Taylors, and issued us a kiss off, like dropping two quarters into a jukebox before walking out a bar to your rhinestoned theme song.

"I'm sorry, but I've got to protect my interests here," he said.

He sauntered off across the grass, toward the tan-sided senior citizen center.

I agonizingly turned to my brother, but Leo just shrugged.

"It'll be okay, man. Maybe we can start up the Bubbles again?"

As condition of going all-in on the Brickhouse Boys, my brother and I had sidelined our project from back home, the Golden Bubbles.

My head spun. I thought back to the magazine, to the nights making music, to my summer in Vermillion. The backfiring pickup, all that had been fed into *this band,* to *this journey.*

Before I could say anything, Donny yelled across the lawn.

"Hey! We gotta go on. They overbooked."

Lawrence doesn't name the band member who accosted him. But he was blindsided and questioned what he meant by "leave."

"We want to leave *you,*" the man shouted. "We're quitting!"

When a nasty Q&A ensued over where they'd leave to, Welk pointed out that Chicago stymied them before.

"You mean *you* couldn't get anything in Chicago!" the mutineer retorted. "We don't want to spend the rest of our lives out here in these sticks. Lawrence, you still bounce around like you're playing at a barn dance, and you can't even speak English!"

The broad-shouldered North Dakota maestro slumped in the

chair. After the band member left, the waitress set down a cup of coffee and a plate of pancakes and asked if anything was the matter, but Lawrence didn't respond. He didn't drink the coffee or eat the pancakes, which in Welk's world, seemed the heaviest of all sins. Then he returned to the hotel, and for the first time in his adult life, Lawrence slept away the afternoon.

───────

"Let's make the last one the best," Monster said, sending a kitty-wampus of sparkles through the tambourine.

I set up my keyboard stand. The other guys plugged into amps on the stage. A crowd of maybe fifty teenagers stared at us. Bobby, on his knees setting up his vocal pedals, grew annoyed about my opened, errant piano case.

"Would you move that?" he asked.

I ignored him, tightening my stand.

"V—I need you to move this stand."

"I'll move it when I move it."

"This is why we can't have a functioning band," Bobby said, his voice rising, "because . . ."

Then the last two weeks, maybe the last two months, or the last twenty years snapped.

"You know what, screw you, Bobby!"

But I didn't say "screw." I said the big word. The word you can't take back. The word that'll rattle around your memory bank like a silver ball bearing in a broken pinball machine the rest of your life.

The band, the crowd, the sound guy all stopped.

They stared at the stage where the tall piano player was yelling at the lead singer. I'm not even sure what all I said, but my voice echoed across the venue, causing the kids to laugh behind muffled hands. The band remained stiff. Bobby just looked at me, stunned.

I had never spoken to him like that. I had never spoken to any-body like that, not even when a lifted pickup tried blowing vaporous carbon in my way as I'd bike along the highway to Mulberry Outlook.

But, somehow, I missed that a smile crossed my lead singer's face.

"Alright," Bobby said, quietly, like a young Kurt Russell in *Tombstone*, finally respecting his arch-nemesis Curly Bill.

It wasn't even that I cursed. It was that, in Bobby's eyes, I could see that he finally saw me as a musician.

"Let's do this," Donny said. "Time's wasting."

We finished sound checking.

"Let's play a mean set," said Monster.

"Yeah, no talking," agreed Poncho. "Just music."

We had thirty minutes on the clock. A row of show kids stood up front. Black stocking caps. Purple jeans. Skater shoes.

"Who are these guys?" I heard a kid ask another. "They're *sick*."

Donny clicked his sticks together—*click, click, click*—and we were off.

Maybe all along Bobby had just been waiting for me to punch back, to show some toughness? Our set was no banter, just songs. The kids threw up limbs, danced, screamed. Donny's sticks hammered the floor toms.

"This symphony" Bobby sang, "is killing me!"

And maybe we weren't obligated to play for them, but the kids drank up our medicine, sweaty-haired and red-splotched faces, these misfits felt together for a matinee, before so many would take flight from Nebraska and never look back.

My hair draped over my keyboard, as our sound filled the senior citizens' cafeteria. At one point I felt a hand playfully rub my head. I looked up to see a grinning Bobby turning back to the crowd to sing the final chorus.

Psychologically, the breakup left Lawrence devastated. Before sleeping in the somber hotel room, however, he proceeded to double down on his monomaniacal dream, setting up the ethos that would create his obstinate run toward a nationally-syndicated television show within two decades.

Years later, a jazz drummer out of Chicago told me, "Welk was a dinosaur. That's why he made it. He wasn't the best. He was just the last one doing it."

And I trace it to Dallas. What happened in Dallas really didn't stay there at all.

"It's curious how we act in moments of personal despair," Lawrence writes in the immediate aftermath of his final performance with the band. "Whenever we put our love and faith into another human being, we are open to hurts and disappointments. That's just part of life."

The Brickhouse Boys packed up our gear and started to load up the van.

"The only one to trust completely is God, and once you can understand that, and learn not to bear any malice or bitterness in your heart, your life will be much happier."

I yelled out, "Hey! Stop! I forgot something."

"I never again took anything quite so personally. I realized that the only important thing in life is to live it as well as you can."

I wasn't positive I had forgotten my power chord. But I wanted to double-check, a small lesson learned. I forgot it so many times already on tour. I ran inside.

"Hey aren't you a Brickhouse Boy?" a kid yelled.

I nodded, pretending this didn't interest in me. On stage, a group of adult men in black leather pants and ripped T-shirts made metal music, and I couldn't help but sense what my parents feared—delayed adolescence. I still couldn't say whether a musician was something I really was or only pretended to be, but I had survived this harebrained tour. I tumbled out the other end.

"We'll get a bigger show this fall, Chris," Bobby said, after the gig. "Promise."

"How about the Corn Palace?" I asked. "There's a good crowd there."

"I've done worse."

Driving home to Vermillion in the ramrodded S.S. *Bly*, the Brickhouse Boys celebrated like mariners returning delirious and punchy from three years chasing a whale.

It felt good knowing we would soon be gone from each other.

"Wish I never had to see this again," my brother said, heaving his bass into his car. "But knowing Poncho, we'll likely play a juvenile delinquent center next Saturday night."

"You boys take care now, you hear!" called Donny.

The old wagon unromantically rumbled away.

We were free.

Leo drove back to Wells. But I had agreed to *South Dakota Magazine* to make up my missed time and blog from the Sturgis Motorcycle Rally, so I drove to the Vice household, where Monster stood on the street corner. He threw his satchel in the back of my Cavalier, and we began our midnight journey to the Black Hills.

Ribbons of black sky overlaid our heads driving westward, two yellow lights our sirens. After 3 a.m., we pulled off to the Triple H gas station in Murdo. Inside, an autographed photograph of Willie Nelson hung on the wall next to glass encasing a leather braid, pants, and tomahawk with a sign: "Props from *Dances with Wolves.*"

Some hucksters and professional drifters in western South Dakota can't get their fill with this film. Somehow, a fake film about a fake man meeting with a fictional American Indian from the post-Civil War frontier still felt relevant to someone twenty years later. Signs advertised cliffs with patches of grass where Costner pointed his cameras. Another billboard on I-90 called drivers to visit a ranch to see horses used in the film. What was weird was not the obsession, but the intermarrying of road and historical signs. From *South Dakota Magazine*, I had learned about Deadwood, a lawless town because the Lakotas wouldn't sell the Black Hills to the United States after Custer had chased gold there. Speculators and prospectors flooded in, leading to wild stories and later books, movies, even an HBO television series. In *Deadwood* the series, murders, shootouts, prostitutes, and hard life is on display, but in focusing on the exaggeration, in pointing out that these myths were created by capitalist foragers, you may forget that something existed.

That week in Saloon No. 10, I stood close to an old black-and-white photograph of a baseball team from 1901, making me think, *dear God, Deadwood had a town ball team?* I spied the second-baseman's mouth, looking for a gold tooth.

From the first chapters of *Wunnerful, Wunnerful,* I felt like every little word had been set down by my own fingers first, turned upside down, stamped with Welk's name, and then right-sided back to my own gaze.

But I was now unsure how much of this guide to trust.

Standing outside the Triple-H, I turned to Monster, who stood bare-legged in jean shorts near the gas corral, with the same Sheriff's shirt on he had worn for three days.

"You ever seen *Dances with Wolves*?"

Monster finished his cigarette.

"I once saw Graham Greene in a hotel in downtown Rapid."

Greene, an Oneida actor, played one of the Lakota leads in the film and had apparently been standoffish to Monster.

"Wouldn't you get sick of people coming up to you, too, though?" I asked.

"Don't be in the movies, then."

Monster raised his hand and pointed at a large, shiny, black van. Men in British voices milled around the gate.

"That's Foreigner's touring van. They're in town for Buffalo Chip."

The jackhammered old bodies in tight black shirts and exposed chest hair and silent-killer boots stood by the glimmering van in the night air. Foreigner. A *real* band.

"Think how many years they've been touring," I asked.

We stared at them for a moment before hopping in the car and driving off into the west, down the interstate further and further. We crossed into the Hills as the purple sun came over our backs, shining the hills for us. As we climbed to the fiberglass Brontosaurus after the sun had risen, Monster told me what it's really like to watch the sun come up out west. But that was a couple of hours away yet. Now it was still dark, except for the floodlights of the Triple-H gas station, and we needed to get out fast, so we floored it; Foreigner were real ghosts, too, as far as we were concerned, as unconnected to the realm of the living as Kevin Costner, a Hollywood western, and that polka king from Strasburg.

INTERMISSION

FIFTEEN-MINUTE UNION BREAK

The fiddle music was supposed to start around 9 p.m., so Carrie and I drove our Prius down an old, one-lane country road till we saw the neon light, "Troubadour," and pulled in somewhere in West Virginia.

It's common, anymore, to be promised a roadhouse in a pop country song and get either a Buffalo Wild Wings-style plastic operation or a parking lot adjacent a watering hole filled with Confederate-flag-waving pickup trucks and "Keep Running Your Mouth, I'm Reloading" bumper stickers.

I'm skeptical of the small town as nobly remembered in today's literature. My hometown watched the hospital close, the club—the Golden Bubble—decay into a meth den, and my parents, public school teachers, get chased out of the municipal liquor store when locals put a quarter in the jukebox to hear Pink Floyd's "Another Brick in the Wall."

But the concierge at the mineral springs hotel had promised us a bluegrass hootenanny, so we drove out. Carrie and I parked the Prius next to a few Econolines—too dark to perceive any bumper stickers—and then walked into the bar, ordered fried cheese curds and a couple of Miller Lites, and eased into the table. Then we waited for the show to begin.

I don't know what's happened to rural America.

Books like J. D. Vance's *Hillbilly Elegy* and Sarah Smarsh's *Heartland* sometimes read like white papers, sometimes like old country songs in different keys, trying to figure out how the dance has changed in small towns and flat-top farms or mountain PO boxes thanks to public spending on agriculture or housing, families or mothers. Vance says, I suppose believably, that he is moved to tears by Lee Greenwood, while Smarsh drops a quarter in a rhinestoned jukebox along a Wichita highway, her grandparents slow dancing near the bar.

But I didn't know that life, exactly. At least not the last part. That wasn't my small-town existence. Mom once drove us two hours north to St. Paul, along the gurgling Mississippi River, to listen to the symphony play Handel's "Water Music" under the conducting of Bobbi McFerrin. I remember a bomb pop pooled in my khaki shorts as we sat in the grass, staring up at the city in the sky above us.

I also remember, closer to home, playing in the Wells Area Community Band at the Faribault County Fair, serenading the pie-eaters with Aaron Copland's "Down a Country Lane" just as the demolition derby entrants growled to a start.

In the early days of writing this book, I attended the South Dakota Festival of Books and stood hard around 8:55 a.m. on a rainy Saturday morning on the cobbled streets nestled into the pine-covered mountains around Deadwood, fiercely debating whether I should attend a session on "emerging novelists" in the historic Franklin Hotel or an old Yankee-road-tobacco-style-seminar in the basement of St. Ambrose Church (oldest parish west of Wall Drug) that focused on "writing about rural South Dakota."

Figuring my book more an essay than a western ghost story, I ducked into the church basement along with two gals using canvas bags to block the rain and took a seat in back as a debate roiled around the demise of six-man football in South Dakota.[1]

---

1. If you don't know, six-man-football is what happens when your high school is large enough to support only three down linemen, a quarterback, a running back, maybe an odd receiver, and a school board with white-knuckled obstinance toward school consolidation with the neighboring county.

As I listened, about how writing about rural South Dakota means being authentic, about roots, about how you can't just have some east coast carpet-baggers coming in and pointing at our taxidermy on the walls of the dentist's office and calling that an observation, I felt my whole body go rigid.

One of the session leaders got chills in the back of his neck when he proclaimed, "I saw the band march past last week and only thirteen kids, maybe three lines, a banged-up snare drum, no one was in step, and a feral cat following up behind, but, darnit, we had a band."

And I thought of my dad, who taught at a small school, but who also asked that kids wear clean spats, who asked that kids shine their horns, who asked that kids stay in line, and march in step, tighten the snare, keep dents out of the tuba, even with the school soon closing after the farm crisis, even with the ceiling tiles leaking.

"A tuba's the price of a good used car," he said, to guffaws. "I'm serious."

Sure, as a rural child I knew the slam of a locker on the weekend when the gun show took over our school, when ten thousand firearms and arrowheads and collectible coins assembled in our hallways and gymnasium.

But I also knew how my classmates urged me to play the piano in the gymnasiums in the morning, how sometimes our middle school choir teacher, to quiet the class, would send me to the front to hear the rubbery bass hand of Vince Guaraldi's "Linus & Lucy."

That night, just south of Berkeley Springs, a bearded guy in a NASCAR cap grabbed the acoustic guitar and walked on stage. Then, a man in a billowy black shirt picked up the bass. Two other guys walked on stage, one holding a fiddle with a bandana tied around his head and the other, a young guy, baby-faced, with a harmonica.

"You take a long enough break?" asked a big boy in front.

The Troubadour had been owned by the radio host out of Winchester, Virginia, who discovered Patsy Cline. They served deep-fat-fried pickles and asked only a couple, wet dollars for a beer. We wondered if the music had gone out of the place.

A trucker-hatted crooner kept circling the island bar, annoying the waitresses, news turned to Fox. At a table near the stage, a table filled with guys in blaze orange ballcaps and jeans, Skol circles embossed onto the back pocket.

"Okay," said the singer, his beard whiskers brushing the microphone. "I think we've given you enough respite."

Then they sang.

Someone might say no one sings along anymore, that the nation no longer holds any songbook. We're divided now, and maybe this is true.

But that night at the Troubadour, that front table sang along to every last bluegrass and country tune they could throw into the air fryer. It wasn't hard, nor ribald. There was melody. Soft, pie-eyed, soaring toward the pines. These boys with calloused hands grew up with all this music. On a Saturday night, mud on their truck tires, fishing lures scratched to visors, they wanted tunes. After the fiddle, they put down beer cans and clapped rough hands together.

Carrie and I stayed for another, before making that short, winding ride back along the cow road, our headlights pivoting at every hairpin curve to flash wanly on some new mysterious pasture, fence, or stone barn, as that car must've done the night Hank Williams died in the backseat, looking for a way down from the mountains.

TIP YOUR BARTENDERS AND SERVERS

My parents started me in on piano at age seven. After years staring at our black upright in the living room, I auditioned for the local piano teacher, Mrs. Jean Carlson, the summer before second grade.

Hopes were high for me, as son of the band director. At night, Mom got a call. "You'll start lessons next fall, Christopher." A small coil sprung up in me.

Is music inherited or not? I think I felt it in me. As a child, kneeling at St. Wenceslaus in Verdigre next to my grandfather, I opened wide my mouth and sang loudly, hoping to impress him. That was how I wanted to play on the piano, too, to learn its language, its literature.

That September, on foggy, cool, leaf-strewn mornings, I biked to Mrs. Carlson's house before school. When snow fell, Mom drove me to the lesson and my teacher's husband gave me a lift to school in his pickup. I would rush into class, beating the bell, my jostling backpack filled with textbooks and the Alfred Beginner Series, dog-eared with pencil scratches in the margins. After two months, I used both hands. After four, my fingers stretched for a fifth. By May, with the lilacs in bloom, snow puddles evaporated from the sidewalk dips, all seemed up to snuff, and I could use those brassy pedals. Both sets of grandparents (except for my mom's dad, Ed, who had died before I was born) drove from the wilds of South Dakota and Nebraska to see my first recital.[22]

I was to perform "Oom-Pa-Pa."

I was terribly nervous.

Waiting in the church pews, my hands shook. The recital proceeded youngest to eldest, so it would ease off in future years. But this year I opened. Promptly at 7:30 p.m. in the Lutheran church, an upside-down boat, my name was called, and before the nervousness could sink in too much, I bounded up and plopped down on the bench, feet barely touching the ground. The Yamaha piano stretched high in front of me, as black as a demure stallion.

Confirmed with self-assured gusto, I plunged in, beginning on G. And immediately, like turning a car key to a dead, frozen engine, what the piano played back to me was wrong. I quizzically looked up at my teacher. Then back down at my hands. Then back up, panicked.

Mrs. Carlson, from the church's pulpit, spoke into the microphone.

"Why don't you try up a fourth, Christopher?"

Laughter murmured behind me.

Determined, heart pounding, I started again. This time on C.

---

2. My Uncle Tommy—illustrating our family's think global, act local philosophy—had bizarrely but effectively always said that, "We buried Dad the same day they shot Anwar Sadat," as if the two events were now hurtling out there in outer space, forever linked.

Initial butterflies calmed as rote, mechanical memory took over. My first solo performance. Within approximately 180 seconds, I cruised to the song's ending with a flourishing triad and was back up in the air, rushing to my pew, to hardy applause, a small Victor Borgia.

One by one, the other kids met their fates. Children played Chopin, Joplin, Debussy. And I smiled, tapping my feet, politely clapping, all the while trying not to swat at the fly of my short-term memory, trying to forget embarrassing myself before the whole town playing wrong notes.

But I couldn't help myself.

It's in these moments that I think of myself as a writer more than a musician, scribbling away notes, trying to understand the self. It's not a selfish act, but it's not the genetics of a musician, who often lives short, who is used up, while the writer continues along, haunted by the past, sitting on the porch, long after the neighbors have gone in, hearing the tunes waft in from a bar downtown with a pang of envy.

After Mrs. Carlson thanked everyone for coming to our recital, we moved into the reception room for cake and coffee in Styrofoam cups. I sat with the other younger pupils, who chatted agreeably, like ski jumpers who had made it to the medal round after a heat. While my parents and grandparents accepted congratulations from our neighbors and local arts patrons on starting their son early in piano, a gnat still pestered me.

Gulping down my cake, I sprinted in my black dress pants and white button-down shirt with an impervious clip-on tie the two blocks home, where I threw the door open and collapsed at the piano, banging out by rote, "Oom-Pa-Pa" multiple times, each time starting on C, never on G, mark it, C, C, C, it never even entering my head to start on G, making me wonder, *why had it*? Why, at the precise time for me to do right, had I instead gone left? How had everything I prepared for been upended by a mindless mistake, as though there had been nothing in my power to avoid the trap sprung for me from moment I'd laid hands on a piano?

Underneath the Jules Breton painting, the woman holding a diminutive scythe, her hair in a bonnet, a sherbet sun furtively peering over a yonder farm, I wonder, too, when will I be done. But there's an old tire, a buried license plate, an oxidized chassis here, if I only can keep digging into the earth.

On that night, that boy kept playing the song, pounding on the white notes, fingers pushing impassionedly into thin keys striking hammers, plucking cables, sending notes skyward like black birds on telephone lines flooding the air after a passing truck's backfire, and within a verse or two, I'm sure his parents and grandparents, walking home, maybe from across the highway, while a purple sky— one of those great prairie storms—threatened, could probably hear their son or grandson pounding, hoping with each repeated song, he would somehow blot out the memory of everything that had just gone wrong.

A SCHOTTISCHE

CHAPTER 18

THE WORLD'S ONLY CORN PALACE IN MITCHELL, SOUTH DAKOTA

SATURDAY, AUGUST 28, 2007

The Corn Palace is basically a golden box. On the outside are murals. Cupolas rise, a flag or two. Maybe a tower. It's all covered in glittering kernels and other antihistamine-agitating boohoo. Like the Taj Mahal and Cabela's. Billboards recklessly call it "the World's Only." At some point, it drew the attention of that blunderbuss, Welk.

You can go one thousand miles in either direction and not see another Corn Palace. And it glows as one of the geographical hotspots where my path overlaps with Welk's, like prehistoric footprints where smaller dinosaurs thousands of years later stepped in bigger dinosaurs' tracks.

After the band broke up, Lawrence and his wife Fern moved to Dallas. Actual Dallas. Not two roads surveyed by a can-munching mule, Dallas (close to Bonesteel, if you're wondering). He gave up music and instead opened a hotel inconspicuously named "The Lawrence."

Without question, catastrophe became this thirty-story shack. Word quickly arrived from a tenant that the building leaked gas. After bursting down a locked door, Lawrence found a resident near-death, collapsed from the fumes, behind a shower curtain in the basement.

Then, predictably, Fern discovered a bootlegging distillery being run out of the hotel by a few tenants. So, Lawrence and Fern left the hotel business, flipping the property for a $17,000 profit. "More than any amount I'd made with the band the last three years," he writes with support from ghostwriter Bernice McGeehan, a real journeyman's journeyman.

Bottomed out, he returned to music in the Midwest. After running a band (and a subsistence chicken farm) in Omaha, Lawrence skated up to St. Paul, points east, and eventually to Chicago.

When the Polka Elvis landed in the Windy City in 1941, he engaged at the Trianon Ballroom, a place he called "the most beautiful ballroom." The Trianon, I can imagine, was a decadent nightmare: wooden dance floor lined with phony Greek colonnade, glossy marble walls imitating Parisian palaces. Cornelius Ward and George Leslie Rapp, the brothers who designed the joint, specialized in movie theaters. But they did ballrooms—and, apparently, corn palaces.

Shrines to agrarian deities once mushroomed across the Midwest: a "corn" palace in Plankinton, a "blue grass" palace in Creston, Iowa, a "grain" palace in Gregory. Enviably, Mitchell boosters, after spending years erecting temporary temples to usher in favorable harvest or cheap tourism dollars, commissioned a permanent palace in 1899. They even found two celebrated Chicago architects, brothers who specialized in gaudy movie theaters.

I'm not sure whether the Rapps visited Mitchell. But the palace was a hit. And beginning in 1947, a former hometown boy with a big city orchestra, saw his name on the golden marquee.

Lawrence loved the joint.

He returned in '51, '57, and twice in the '60s.

So did my relation, Edna Stoner, who lay in bed at the base of the stage, staring up at the show with her bright eyes.

Edna's tale came to me through Grandma when I was still very young. Basically, in the 1920s, South Dakota had two things going for it: it wasn't yet the Dust Bowl of the 1930s, when Black Blizzards clogged up most municipalities for a decade, and it was the halcyon days of the barn dance circuit.[1]

As the tall tale goes, a young woman, Delores and her sister Marie, before she met and married her quiet German farmer, used to attend ladies night at the Ritz south of Beresford, where they would run into Edna.

Edna was the cousin of my Grandpa Ed (who dropped out of Creighton after a year to help run the farm), and she garnered a profile as a frequent dancer at the Hotsy Totsy Boys shows. But this Stoner girl came down with mysterious, debilitating arthritis, and would never dance around the wooden, shiny dance floors again.

"She was a gimp" Grandma told me, using language we wouldn't anymore.

Nevertheless, Edna struck up a letter-writing campaign to Welk. We don't know what was in those letters, but her words made such an impression on Welk, that late in his career—when he had ABC by the jugular and everyone knew him to carry a big stick as America's Band Leader—he played the World's Only Corn Palace and invited Edna as his special guest.

Again, the details were stitched together from variant versions lulled by smoking aunts with lipstick on Styrofoam coffee cups at midnight while I slept face down on the big wooden table in Grandma's kitchen, but I recall that when the day arrived, the Stoners lifted Edna and the bed into the back of a truck and freighted her the one hundred miles to Mitchell for the big show.[2]

---

1. By "barn-dance circuit," I mean: *dance hall dance hall every Saturday night*, getting in trouble at church the next morning, sneaking flasks into hootenannies, Model T's with upside-down chiffon dresses out by the lake, haylofts with fiddlers, European accordionists, small towns come for an afternoon/stay bored for a lifetime, cow pastures, and rampant peach Schnapps. Basically what was going on in *The Great Gatsby* with Carraway, Tom, Daisy, and the crowd, but instead of wherever the hell they held their blacked-out, shimmering nights, they held them here on the dusty prairie in emptied barns and Carnegie-endowment dance halls.
2. It may've been an ambulance, but I distinctly remember a pickup, and I see her on the highway, her hair a-flutter, a nephew staring out the back of the pickup, "We'll be there soon, Edna, we're almost there," and then the Corn Palace emerging in the distance.

There, a photograph was snapped, and whenever my mom and her siblings visited the Stoner residence, someone pointed to the picture of Welk standing bedside with glittering Champagne ladies and said, "Here's a photo with Lawrence Welk and Edna in bed."

No one, of course, laughed until a good hundred yards removed from the premises. They didn't mean *that* kind of "in bed."

But prepositions can be tricky.

And Grandma—clutching the small, golden crucifix dangling from her neck—laughed midstory, never able to finish, as my mother or aunt put me on her shoulder and carried me upstairs.

The Brickhouse Boys did play the Corn Palace. Let's get that straight.

"A band bailed," Bobby said. "And they called us."

For that Saturday, the S.S. *Robert Bly* was cleaned and smelling of fake plastic pine trees. Donny vacuumed obliterated Cheetos, removed tossed-off empty cans of Dew. The miniature fan hoisted on a suction cup even worked again.

Better news, we had a great opener: "Weird Al" Yankovic.[3]

Technically we played on the street outside the Corn Palace aboard a flatbed. But in my own way, I had somehow made it.

Under a sky blue, on a late August Saturday, Weird Al released his hordes out of the Maize Temple. The crowds flooded the streets. We fired up covers.

"Like a tiny liiiiitle penny crawling up the piiipe," sang Bobby, supporting our version of Amy Winehouse's "Back to Black."

A jolly caramel corn manufacturer bobbed his head while sliding his spoon through the silver vat; a few maudlin teens stared at us stone silent, while their ready-to-go dads folded arms and twirled thin key fobs. On the flatbed trailer, graced by a large American flag, Bobby sang from his knees, Donny wiped sweat from his folded brow with one hand while keeping the stick on his hi-hat, my brother paddled his Squire, Monster box-stepped like a Casanova while holding

---

3. No relation to Frankie.

down a single note on the hockey-toothed keyboard, Poncho pulled static rain from his theremin, and I slung piano-rock hash out on Kurt, my long black board spread over an X-stand on the center of that stage beneath the hulking Corn Palace. I felt the band as a singular presence underneath those golden domes of agrarian Byzantium, and I looked out to the crowd—moms and dads, denim-panted grandparents, surly teenagers and rambunctious children, watching us with curiosity and then waning interest—only to see our crowd slowly disappear.

Soon more key fobs emerged. Parents ushered kids to the parking lot. There had been a brief hiatus of the triage during our covers, but when we returned to our originals, a steady stream of black SUVs met our report on the road out of town.

"We had those suckers for a song or two!" Donny called, spinning his drumsticks on his knuckles like pinwheels.

"Maybe we need a new song?" I responded, lugging my keyboard down the ramp to the van.

Donny took off his sweaty V-neck and reached for his cigarettes. "They just don't get us."

I shuddered.

As we packed up in the shadow of the Corn Palace, I stared up at the hieroglyphics of a band playing in the cornhusks, and like a thick *Riverside* Shakespeare to the head, I suddenly realized Welk would never say that.

It was our job to get *them*.

When we got back to Vermillion that night—well past midnight—I dropped my shirt in the bathroom and took a cold shower in the bathtub with gold-clawed feet, washing off the night's gig.

Standing on stage in Mitchell, for the first time I felt an obligation to the crowd. Maybe they didn't get us. Maybe they didn't listen to Jeff Buckley or memorize the lines to *High Fidelity*. But in the scheme of things, South Dakotans had big-screen televisions and movies and surround sound in their SUVs to return to. They had options for entertainment. And if we were going to work, to play for the people, we needed to give them something worth standing around for.

Toweling off, I threw on shorts, turned on my piano, and kept all the lights off, while the blue glow of the keyboard's LCD display screen hauntingly washed my face. And I went looking for a song.

Part of the beauty of the Brickhouse catalog had been its rejected status. It had been scraps of tunes that found a home with us. But writing a song is a mystery. It never happens the same way. You know how they show it in biopics—where the crooner slams the truck bed after getting dumped by his girlfriend, grabs his guitar, and writes out a melody?

That's rarely how it happens.

But it's *sometimes* how it happens. When you need a song, really need an answer back from beyond, it'll find you. But it requires mindlessness. You'll start dropping hands. Three or four gloomy notes on the piano, hoping for a nice-sounding mistake. Then comes a rhythm, a groove. A melody. It's humming first, then words. Or maybe just an idea. Then, frantically, like people crashing a wedding, the chorus rushes in, mad and looking for a drink. Maybe you accidentally repeat the quarter-note whole-step up to an E, and soon, like a chainsaw carving taking first shape out of the haze, the flying splinters, choking sawdust, something comes visible like a pirate or a garden gnome with a sneering lip, or maybe that Private George Shannon who'd gone missing on Lewis and Clark's trip west.

That night, I caught a glimpse of Beethoven's "Fur Elise" and our touring van. And a tune came to me. Like making love or throwing a baseball after years away, you rely on muscle memory with songwriting. Its creation is bound up in your extremities and mechanics. There's no brain in songwriting. I've met plenty of fools who are musicians. That's almost, in fact, a prerequisite: a foolish consistency to whittle away on the porch with a guitar through shower storms and thunderclouds, looking for that song.

While I played that night, a thunderclap overhead, outside town on the southern perimeter, the creek would be filling up. The thirsting, June dirt would suck up the water droplets, growing the grass and crops and stems of weeds, and the dopey cows standing solitary in the pasture would barely nod as the silver droplets pelted their furry heads.

And when I was done, pulling off my headphones at the keyboard, I saved the song on my laptop's GarageBand and named the track, "Waterloo (War Song)," convinced this song was the sound of our band breaking up.

CHAPTER 19

THIRD FLOOR, I. D. WEEKS LIBRARY, UNIVERSITY OF SOUTH DAKOTA

THURSDAY, SEPTEMBER 13, 2007

Graduate school started a week later, so after sleeping in, showering, putting on chinos, and waiting for the tinning in my ear to stop, I sat in class as our English professor told us "reality is language-based."

"Often when we size up a book," said Dr. Emily Hader, "what we're trying to find is where the book breaks down, where the mythology of the book unravels. Find a loose thread, and pull."

I had forgotten our summer assignment, to pick a novel to study. Scrambling for a title, as Dr. Hader went around the room, I called out all I could think of.

"This Welk autobiography?"

She cocked her head, giving her ponytail a jangle.

Ice swelled in my veins. This was a serious, academic class. My Harvard-educated professor might point to the door and ask that I go hand in my student loan check.

But Dr. Hader was a cool customer.

"When my husband volunteered to work the phone banks at the public television station," she said, wryly, "You would not *believe* how many requests asked to keep *The Lawrence Welk Show*."

So began the third phase of my project.

Reading the book was different this time. Before, I leisurely passed through a photo album. Now I dug through a shoebox of Polaroids.

Growing up I heard sordid rumors from my family. Worst came from my dad's sister, Jenny, and her husband, Ted, who lived in Yankton across the street from a home once lived in by Welk.

"One night," Ted would say, "Lawrence skipped town with his wife, child, and a bag of cash in tow."

Somehow, that detail hovered, and reading *Wunnerful, Wunnerful* for a third time, a phrase caught my eye.

In the Dakotas, Welk used to supplement gigs by selling Honolulu Fruit Gum,[1] but when he lost the sponsorship, the barn dance Brahms moved to Omaha, where—he writes—the population was "ten times what it was in Yankton." Fine, whatever. What drew my attention was almost an afterthought: Lawrence writes that he and Fern "almost immediately" moved "bag and baggage" to Omaha.

I took a sip of my microwaved tea and sat up on the futon at 123 Forest Avenue.

Sold it almost immediately?

I walked over to my desk, laid the book flat out against the bright lantern, and placed my trembling fingers on the page. What was this, this "almost immediately?" A simple "we moved to Omaha" would've sufficed.

But "almost immediately?"

I flipped back a few pages, read another sentence, and stared off through the storm window, past the woolly oak outside the sleeping suite, down into the empty concrete street where water drained into the culvert buried under the bluff.

It was so obvious, so devastating; this was some kind of coverup.

Watching *The Lawrence Welk Show* you can see it: pleasantness, happiness, escape.

Victor Greene's *The Passion of Polka* (a book he admittedly wrote because—living in blue-collar, sausage-downing Milwaukee—he

---

1. Hence, Delores's tales of silver bubblegum wrappers strewn over the Ritz's floor.

couldn't not), describes "Polka Happiness" as the overall effect of the music.

A lot of polka plays off of self-deprecation. There's the "Too Fat Polka" by Frankie Yankovic and the Yanks, featuring the winning chorus, "She's too fat. She's too fat. She's too fat for meeeee," which seems to plead guilty to pot-calling-the-kettle-black misgivings. Then there's the "Just Because" polka, in which the lovesick protagonist laments his romantic interest's penchant for calling him "Old Sant-y Clause." Finally, there's "In Heaven There Is No Beer," which is the major premise in a syllogism we don't need to finish.

But what happens when this façade fails—in even the tiniest spot?

Under the tawny light of my desk lamp, other lines of text popped. Like Welk's critical take on the Lennons, his popular sisterly quartet. "I would have been glad to do so if only they had asked," he writes, about letting the gals out of contracts.

Oh come on, Lawrence, *really*?

Then there was chapter 20, "Champagne Music Makers," wherein Lawrence tells the story about how he poured a drink on his lap, unfamiliar with using a swizzle stick.

"I went to scarlet with embarrassment and thought, 'Well, dummer-Esel, you've done it again!'"

Big deal. That's credibility in large swaths of the American interior.

Another night, in an online rabbit hole, I read that Welk fired Champagne Lady Alice Lon on live TV for wearing a cheesecake skirt. In the book, Welk pleads, "Outside influences began to make her dissatisfied."

Please.

Soon, I approached the book like a prosecuting attorney. When he talked about the revolving door of Champagne Ladies, I couldn't help but notice him referring to one replacement as "the tallest, skinniest girl" he'd ever seen, and "downright plain," and a—if I have the words correct (and I do)—"plucked chicken."

There were even plain factual errors, such as when he visited a Catholic priest and the priest's *wife* in Decatur, Illinois, or when he crashed that bus in a gully headed to "Estherville, Ohio," which, according to Google Maps, doesn't exist.

These discrepancies, mind you, weren't big. But they weren't tidy copyediting errors, either.

Weeks into the semester, sitting on my front porch, sipping Capri Sun, I unloaded my nascent theory on Collette.

"Lawrence Welk, a jerk?" she asked, stunned by my reversal. "Come on!"

"No," I maintained, jutting out my chin. "It's all brain science now. How else would he get so famous!?"

"Maybe hard work!" Collette said. "What, he's a jerk because he once ate only pickles to save money on a long road trip with his wife?"

It was a bitter pill, admittedly.

"Famous people are selfish," I said. "Serial killers and rock stars share the same brain."

By November, my advisor, Professor Skip Wilson, a shaven-headed critical theory professor and North Dakotan who loved the Cure, told me to submit my research to a pop culture conference in New Mexico.

Two weeks later, I heard back.

"Hey!" Skip said, leaning back in his armchair in front of a Bono poster. "That's great news. Maybe Lawrence Welk can be your thing."

I took a sip of my Dr. Pepper, and tried to think fondly about this sentence.

CHAPTER 20

A HOTEL CONFERENCE ROOM IN ALBUQUERQUE, NEW MEXICO

SATURDAY, FEBRUARY 16, 2008

The night before Valentine's Day, I drove to Kansas City. Then, in the morning, I put in my CD of Beirut's new album and drove west, past windmills and old-century barns. Kansas looked like Mars with grass seed. By Liberal, my CD player stopped working. I could no longer feel the seat of my pants by Amarillo. So I got out to smell the gasoline spewed by the El Caminos circling town. I finally plunged past those watermelon-rock mountains late into Albuquerque.

That next morning, I visited an old Franciscan church.

"Hello?" I asked, walking into the gift shop.

A woman with white hair and glasses draped over her shirt smiled. Her blue eyes lit up when she saw me.

"Why hello!"

We chatted, and I told her about my conference.

"We watched him every Saturday night," she smiled. "You should go see the Lennons in Branson. See anything you like?"

A glass case held an array of silver medals.

"Do you have any of Saint Christopher?"

He was the patron saint of travelers, and after journeying so long, I felt in need of protection.

The woman unlocked the case and roped a thin chain around her finger.

"You know he's not a saint anymore?"

"What?"

"The Vatican said the story about him—that he'd carried a boy on his shoulders across a river, and when they reached the other side the boy had grown into Christ—was far too much speculation."

"Well, that's a bummer."

The old woman ruefully smiled at me, like one reveals a secret.

"Not all saints get to stay saints," she said, philosophically.

The medal cost me $19.99.

Studying a book, letting language and ideas soak into your pores, is an act of scholarship, but it's also an emotional process. And sometimes, we're not ready to part.

On Saturday morning, I walked into my panel's room before anyone else. I sat down, took out my ten-page paper, and poured myself a glass of water from the carafe. *What a 180 this had been.*

Since the band's demise, I had come to enjoy the quiet, organized atmosphere of libraries, lecture halls, and campuses at dark. *This was just the beginning*, I daydreamed at the dais. *My talk in New Mexico would be the first of many academic appearances, and after presenting today* . . . I glanced at the clock (10:03 a.m.), wondering when my fellow presenters would arrive and . . . 10:03 a.m.?

We were supposed to start at 10 a.m.

The room was still empty.

Quickly, I jogged down the carpeted corridor. Crowds filled conference rooms. Session titles hung near doors:

"The Grateful Dead as Shakespearean Fool."

"*Firefly* and Cultural Entropy."

"Common vs. Kanye."

Turning around mid-stride, I ran back to my room and checked my room's placard.

Christopher Vondracek, "Slavoj Zizek's Multicultural Aestheticism and Three Christmas Specials from The Lawrence Welk Show"—along with three other panelists who hadn't shown up.

Like Lawrence in Hague, it hit me: *nobody would be coming.*

The conference room walls throbbed. I sat back down, steadying myself, staring at the empty chairs, sipping water from my cup.

Make Lawrence Welk your thing! Skip had said.

The world couldn't care less.

I realized it'd be a long drive home. If I started now, I could reach Denver by sundown.

Standing up, I took off my lanyard, stuffed *Wunnerful, Wunnerful* into my bag, and pushed in my chair, when a knock sounded at the doorway.

"Hello?"

A woman with curly black hair and green glasses waved.

"Is this the Lawrence Welk talk?"

Many observers believe *The Lawrence Welk Show* was only popular in the Midwest, but in *Ah-One and Ah-Two,* his second book, the plot revolves around when he sold out Madison Square Garden in the 1970s.

I could pull ratings from any month, but let's just say July 1957. That month, only one ABC show landed in the top-ten of the Nielsen ratings, next to *Ed Sullivan, Alfred Hitchcock,* and *Gunsmoke*: *The Lawrence Welk Show.*

As *Look Magazine* wrote, "nobody likes him but the people."

I gestured to the empty chairs, a table devoid of panelists.

"Where is everyone?" the woman replied.

"No one showed," I said, pouring myself another glass. "I must've chosen the wrong thing to write about."

The woman zigzagged between brown folding chairs, her black unbuttoned sweater over her black dress shirt flowing like an extravagant cape.

"What do you mean, wrong thing?" she asked, pushing up her glasses. "Like, wrong topic?"

"No one showed up to my talk," I said. "It reminds me of that saying, *if a tree falls in the forest and no one is there to . . .*"

"*I'm* interested in Lawrence Welk."

She jested.

"I teach theater in California, and when I saw your paper title, I got excited. You know that show was more influential than people realize."

"Seriously? I mean, *yes*, I say the same thing in my . . ."

"Would you read it to me?"

She removed a notepad from her satchel and caught me flat-footed with her directness.

"Well, I don't know if," I stammered. Then I breathed deeply. "Happily," I said, anxiously scooping my paper and sitting down.

"Okay, so Welk was underappreciated by critics, right?"

And the show began.

It's awkward, reading. Unlike piano, I don't lose myself. No one really enjoys themselves while you talk. They listen to your words. Pay attention to your socks. But in the inkling of this story, I felt the beginnings of a real project.

"I guess Welk's tragedy was that he believed in American entrepreneurialism. But companies advertising on his show—Pontiac, Geritol—went bust. They'd offshore, tear up the factories dotting that ring of cities from Pittsburgh to Milwaukee along the Great Lakes, which was his greatest bedrock, the Rust Belt, the Polka Belt. No more accordions," I said.

"No more accordions," she repeated, nodding.

"But you have to believe that for millions of Americans each week, he was the only live music they'd see. 'Live' of course is relative. But he brought music into homes. You know, Lawrence had a rule that he wouldn't perform to audiences smaller than the number of people in his band."

My lone audience member grinned, taking notes, her face down, causing her to frequently push her horn-rimmed glasses up the bridge of her nose.

"Guess, we're at a standoff, then."

"We are," I said. "Let me show you something."

I opened to the glossy photographs in the middle and held up the book.

"This is my grandpa's cousin: Edna."

The eyes behind the black frames smiled.

"Hello, Edna."

"There's some family legend about them involving a misplaced preposition."

I set the book aside and moved soberly to the conclusion.

"Finally, there are these Christmas Specials."

The Dodge Dart sitting under the Christmas Tree struck me as symbol for the loss of one kind of American identity.

"That's what Welk overlooked: the country was changing. Not because of outside forces, but because of the very one—capitalism— he so loved."

She applauded.

"Bravo!"

I fake bowed from my seat.

"Thank you. I'll be here for another five minutes. Any questions?"

"How'd you first get into Welk in the first place?"

"Shoot, that's a tough one."

Walking down the hallway, I buttoned up my coat and told her an abridged version.

"You're in a band?" she asked, clarifying.

"I was. I started finding all these stories that matched my own, troubles with the van, groupies, shady venues, even ending up in the same small towns, albeit eighty years removed."

She adjusted her bookbag straps and stopped.

"Why don't you write about that?"

"I don't know," I murmured. "That doesn't sound very, um, historical."

"So, everyone who cares about that television bandleader is dead or just about dead, right? And, trust me, fewer will have the stomach for what you just said, all that technical, Marxist jargon that you mentioned."

I blushed.

"And I think it's pronounced *histrionics*, not *hysterics*."

I blushed again.

"But your band, and that Edna woman, you've got a story there."

I stood chagrined in the lobby, clutching my coat.

"What would the story be, though? He got famous and we didn't?"

She pivoted toward the lobby.

"Can I buy you coffee?"

One of the unexpected benefits to my work has been I always get to hear the little stories that people have tied to Welk. He was only on in the background, but curiously everyone remembers him because they were often near people they loved who are no longer around.

"The thing I loved most about watching *The Lawrence Welk Show* every Saturday night with my family was the Lennon Sisters. Their dresses. Their singers. Their dancing. My sisters and I wanted to be them!"

For a second, I thought of my mother and her sisters, who used to watch the shows.

"That's why I came to find your talk today," she confessed.

The atrium flurried with scholars hustling around and between us.

"Well, I'm glad I could help," I stammered.

"Good luck," she said, shaking my hand. She walked past the coffee bar and called out.

"Who would write about Lawrence Welk! How wonderful!"

I walked out to the parking lot.

Driving north through the mountains of northeastern New Mexico, purple shadows crawled around patches of snow and sage brush and ranch fence. Dusk fell north of Pueblo and into Denver. Around midnight, I pulled off at a Motel 6 just into Nebraska, back in my father's homeland. I woke up to growling semi-trucks, words and music rattling in my brain.

CHAPTER 21

SEBASTIAN JOE'S ICE CREAM PARLOR, MINNEAPOLIS, MINNESOTA

SATURDAY, JUNE 23, 2008

That next summer, I found myself in Minneapolis, living in the basement of a friend's house along Bde Maka Ska.

The Throwback drove in the *Bly* across the country. Leo and I played a few shows with our band, the Golden Bubbles. But I had to finish a draft of my Welk project before my last year of graduate school. Whenever I came up for light, my roommates, St. Olaf graduates, asked, "What's going on down there?"

I would mumble "working" and then descend.

In truth, I didn't know what I was doing. I didn't have a job. I definitely wasn't writing much. And I slept on an air mattress, watching *Ice Road Truckers*. Other than a few articles about fans in Queens nursing homes, the world had stopped caring about Welk the moment he died. No fossils in the rock record.

One night, taking a break, I met up with Uncle Bill and his wife Mary at an ice cream parlor.

"Oh, we watched the show," Bill said. "We were forced to."

"It was like a religion," said Mary.

I told them I had suspicions that Welk had actually not played by the rules and was more mischievous than he let on.

"Maybe that Edna Stoner story isn't so crazy," said Mary.

Spoons clinked in the ice cream dishes.

"Oh Mary," Bill said.

"*Your* family told me the story."

"What story?" I asked.

Mary looked from me to Bill.

"Fine, go ahead . . ."

Mary lowered her voice.

"You know the story on Edna . . ."

"Edna was bedridden and Welk struck up a friendship with her, and . . ."

"No, the *real* story."

A flutist in my mind held a long, solitary note.

"No?"

The cicadas in the eucalyptus-like trees *see-see-saaawed.*

"Aunt Edna," Mary whispered, "was bedridden *because* of Welk."

Rain began to fall.

"I don't get it."

Mary leaned in close, staining the stucco walls by pronouncing every last, dirty syllable,

"Syphilis."

CHAPTER 22

THREE MILES SOUTH OF BERESFORD, SOUTH DAKOTA

DECEMBER 25, 1951

The Ritz Ballroom went up in flames on Christmas Night, 1951. The fire started somewhere in the eaves. The interior crackled to hundreds of degrees. The dance floor burned last.

"That's the way a lot of them went up," a Minneapolis dentist, whose parents ran the dance hall in Centerville, South Dakota, told me in an interview. "Mysteriously."

In its heyday, the Ritz Ballroom reigned supreme.

On a clear night, the cornfields glowing amber, men strolled into the Ritz in linen topcoats bought from tailors in Sioux City; they stood in the grass, putting brown bottles to lips, watching as women in powdered noses rode Studebakers like royalty into this crow yard and hoisted themselves up from vehicles with their clutch hand, careful not to step in standing water.

By 9 p.m., electric bulbs in the ballroom burst into an alphabet of heat and white-hot twinkle in the scummy air. Multiple hits on the snare drum. *Snap, snap, snap.* Vibrations shook loose wire strands. Does sprinted along the gully a few miles south of the Ritz, pointed toward the state line. A farmer doffed his cap after tying up the mare, almost able to hear the groan of engines mixed with the squeal of a cornet player running scales in the dusk.

Charlie flipped open his lighter, "That fella's got his eye on you."

Edna loved to dance. Tall and slender, with a sideways smile, she knew about the Ritz, the streamers dipped from wooden masts with weak beer served in back. Maybe she sneaked in, or maybe she assisted the band, lugging equipment. Either way, she was there, behind velvet ropes, on hot dust floors, waiting to join. Maybe the bandleader saw her blue eyes and black hair, her sloping cheek bones, her slender arms.

"May I have this dance?"

And they would be off. Round and round the dance floor, the couple gyrated. Locals cupped mouths in astonishment at their speed, their grace.

"Is that Victor Stoner's daughter?"

The thickness of her calves, the power and precision in his hands and shoulders. Even Lawrence—quite a handful himself—beat back fatigue. He hadn't danced this way since he was a kid at those three-day weddings.

But is this how it happened?

In *Mister Music Maker,* author Mary Lewis Coakley interviews Edna, who describes waking up one morning with shooting back pain. Her hand, involuntarily, turned in on itself. Her fingers broke. Soon her feet, too, almost cloven-toed turned inward. She was rushed to Sioux Falls and returned with braces on her legs. They burst overnight, the pain excruciating.

No doctors, no specialists, priests, or prayers could save her. The family waited for her to die in the Sioux Falls hospital. But, miraculously, she didn't. She returned from the edge. She would never walk again. But she was alive.

The family set her up a four-post brass bed, an island of home-healthcare in the living room. Near her, an oxygen tank hummed in a black, serpentine coil. Her father, Victor, a fix-it man, made bird feeders and worked on the rail across the street from the church. Edna had a view of a backyard, of hills east of town, of the church.

She also had radio. Each night, the family would listen to music.

After Lawrence matriculated from the Dakotas, he hit up hotels in St. Paul, Chicago, Milwaukee, and beyond. In Pittsburgh, at the William Penn Hotel in the 1930s, his band first appeared nationwide. The signal carried from the ballroom, to the radio tower, and finally to a home in Beresford.

Often, Maggie rotated the dial for Edna. Fancy bands, far away. Silver platters, steak knives, muted cornets, and calypso beats. One night, a signal dropped silvery from the sky:

Tonight, ladies and gentlemen, from the William Penn Hotel and the Italian Terrace Room, here in downtown Pittsburgh, Pennsylvania, Steel City, we're happy to bring you a new orchestra that Si Steinhauer, the polka king-maker, is just raving about. Please welcome back Lawrence Welk and His Champagne-Music-Makers!

And in her bones a pulsing.

"Mother . . ." she called. "Mom!!"

A crash of plates. Boarders peered from the dining room through the French doors. Maggie ran in.

"Edna, what is it?"

"Listen!"

The soft, golden strains descended like a man holding a plate of sausages waltzes down stairs.

Ba-bu-bump-bu-bump.
Do-do-do-Do-do-do-Do-Do-Do-Do.
La la la la
"The Pennsylvania polka!"

Victor hopped atop the stairs on one foot.

"Ladies? Is everything okay!?"

His wife looked to their daughter and rushed over to hold her hands, seeing Edna's head rising from the bed-sheets with a smile, her eyes with tears.

When the Ritz burned, its ashes mixed with snow. In the 1930s, four thousand men had packed shoulder-to-shoulder to hear participants in the Farmers' Holiday movement speak. Speakers wired up outside the Ritz aired the speeches to another six thousand gathered. Milo Reno, an activist, yelled out, "Let's eat our wheat and ham and eggs. They can eat their gold!"

The roadhouse complemented the land, becoming a diner, a movie theater, a landmark.

But now it said goodbye. The façade of the wooden dancehall would've been lit like a drunk Christmas tree. Maybe a farmer phoned in the fire department? Men dropped saucers filled with Irish cream and liquor, put on wool coats, and rushed to the station. Maybe they thought about their youth—kisses behind the fence, when they watched that famous polka man from Yankton float in on a cloud?

Smoke maybe reached Edna's window, sleeping under the Welk memorabilia, under that photograph of her at the Corn Palace hanging on the dark, stubbornly immovable wall.

CHAPTER 23

ON THE ROAD FROM HURLEY,
SOUTH DAKOTA

SATURDAY, OCTOBER 13, 1981

The first thing I did was call Mom.

For a day, I stormed around my basement, circling the blow-up mattress, staring with futility at my laptop, fuming.

This was the only plot that made sense. I long suspected something insidious lurked in Welk's closet. His band got famous, ours didn't.

"So did Welk give syphilis to Edna?" I asked.

"Christopher," she said, "The poor Stoner family would die to hear this."

"But is it true?"

"Christopher, it's just a story!"

"But then how'd she get bedridden?"

Mom spoke as though she told me the color of the sky.

"She had rheumatoid arthritis."

The gullibility lodged in my throat. I felt silly. I chased Welk for nearly an entire year . . . to, what, to find out some crummy joke? That I'd fallen for some old family legend?

I thanked her for her time, businesslike, but Mom—in her teacher's voice—had more to say.

"You know, Christopher," she said, "I think Dad and I talked about Lawrence Welk on our first date."

"What?" I laughed. "Seriously?"

And I could see it, the blue Chevette zipping northward on Highway 19 past dry stalks of October corn out of Hurley. The sun swells reddish gold the gray line of corn, the earth so flat you might be able to see the crust curve. Inside that car are two teachers. The band director, Chuck Taylors and suede canvas suit coat, mustache, Jackson Browne hair. The English teacher, his date, with a puff of black hair, thin nose, cobalt eyes, and red lipstick. It's a Saturday night. They're headed to Mitchell for a show. George is nervous. They're the same age, about twenty-three or twenty-four, but he's already in his third year. The faded AM radio crackles in. He's cleaned out the ashtray, though he rarely smokes. An Econoline barrels past them in the opposite direction, the football team is out of town, and George asks for clarity.

"How was he related to you again?"

"Who? Welk?"

"Yeah, the Polka Elvis."

CHAPTER 24

MILLTOWN, SOUTH DAKOTA

SATURDAY, SEPTEMBER 23, 2015

My project went quiet for a few years. I moved home to Minnesota to teach at a college above the Mississippi River. My brother moved to Minneapolis to make music and deliver pizzas. The band scattered.

Sure, I wrote and rewrote drafts, popped by itinerant moments of research. In Chicago on a cool, fall day in 2011, I visited the pink Edgewater Hotel & Resort, where Lawrence—as promised to Fern—landed his orchestra. But I only found an octogenarian in a neon tracksuit, running circles in the parking lot.

On a frigid winter's Saturday a few years later, I drove to Fargo to visit the North Dakota State University Archives, filing through a temperature-controlled diary kept by Welk's youngest sister, who pasted newspaper clippings Fern mailed home.

But I didn't know what I wanted. Mostly, I read his books: 1974's *Ah-One, Ah-Two*; 1976's *My America, Your America*; 1979's *This I Believe*; and 1981's *You're Never Too Young*. The quality of texts dropped after the first couple. Later efforts get dragged into calls to repeal child labor laws and replace the Supreme Court with something called "The Blue Ribbon Committee." It's mostly unreadable.

But I didn't work as a journalist. I tended in my own head, away from people, in libraries or in coffee shops.

And that was a mistake if I wanted the story of Welk.

Luckily, after years of teaching, I returned to the Missouri.

In May 2015, I attended a wedding in Yankton. The reception was at the Rosebud Brewery near the river. During the dance, I spotted my old friends from *South Dakota Magazine*.

"Been a long time, Chris," said the editor, Bernie, shaking my hand.

"Hey, Chris," said his daughter, Katie.

They were just the people I wanted to see. I figured, if nothing else, I'd try to parlay my Welk research into a standalone story on dance halls.

"Anyone ever covered those gems?" I asked.

"You gotta talk to Sherwin Linton," Katie said. "He's a cowboy singer."

"I think he even got some votes for president back in 1980," said Bernie.

When I returned to St. Paul, I phoned up Linton, wearer of ten-gallon hats and a booming crooner. I asked him what happened to the rock n' roll scene, to the dance halls. Sherwin was point blank.

"Marijuana," he said. "All these long-haired hippies came in during the seventies, and they didn't want to dance. They just sat on the floor and got high."

If I wanted to get to the bottom to the dance hall disappearance, Sherwin said, I would need to talk to Myron Lee. When he asked why I was interested in this story, I told him I used-ta-be a musician.

"You *used-ta-be* a musician?" Sherwin bellowed on the phone. "Don't tell me you *used-ta-be* anything."

A week or so later, I chatted with the lead singer of Myron Lee & the Caddies, the first rock n' roll band in Sioux Falls. Myron told me about opening for the Rolling Stones at a rural Texas county fair.

"So, I guess, err, what happened to the music scene in South Dakota?"

"What do you mean what happened?"

"You make it sound so great, but it seems gone now. Like it's like these dinosaurs just disappeared in the rock record. Where'd the music go?"

"Weed," he told me.

"Really?" I asked. "Sherwin said the same thing."

"Oh," Myron replied, "He'd know."

Myron's big hit, "Roger Rabbit," with a chorus that goes, "Roger Rabbit, Roger Rabbit, Roger Raaaaaabit," was recorded at a lakeside studio in Okoboji, Iowa. It wasn't fine art, but his was a dance band. The Caddies played ballrooms. Tickets were one dollar. Concessions included candy and watery 3.2 beer. Fistfights in the parking lot commenced at midnight.

"My senior year I made more than my English teacher," he bragged.

"Not much changes," I said, now years into teaching English. "Thanks for your time."

"One more thing, Christopher," he said, gravelly voiced. "If you're going to write this story, and you're just a pup so I don't know how you're going to write this story, but you really should visit Milltown. That was one helluva dance hall. You'll really feel it visiting there."

On the last Saturday night in September, I drove from St. Paul in a suit-coat and jeans to Milltown, an hour west of Sioux Falls on the James River, the longest non-navigable stream on the continent. Gas station hot-dog wrappers lay crumped on my dashboard. Wind piercing golden ears of corn slipped into my cracked-open windows.

Using the coordinates from the email, I pulled up to a house where an older woman watched a corn maze.

"Two customers out there right now," she said, maintaining her gaze. Gourds hung from tree branches. "John-boy's on his way."

Soon, a pickup ambled up the gravel road. Her fifty-five-year-old son pulled up with mud-speckled sunglasses.

"Well, get in," he said. "I'll show you something."

Milltown is now just a grassy lot near the river. The old main street hides under thin, concrete foundations of ghost homes. A rickety bridge connects the island to the mainland.

"Where's the dance hall?" I asked.

"Didn't Myron tell you?" John asked. "National Guard bulldozed it. Flood hazard. Milltown stood until about the '90s. People came from all around. Great bands. Great parties. Sometimes kids took their daddy's car and drove in reverse on the way home to hide the miles."

"But what happened?"

Two men stood near plastic buckets along the river, fishing.

"People wanted to save it," said John, shifting into drive, "But I told them, *those times aren't coming back!*"

It had stayed on my mind for years, whether a sapping of spirit, a draining of demographics, a collapsing of dance halls had been manifested by the absence of a Welk figure of our current age. Maybe Welk had been a lark, a singular *jouissance* produced by a fertile mid-country forever wrecked, halved, in-decline?

But I had come to see a natural process. It had been a season. Life had flourished, like in the spring. Grown. Dried up. Harvested. And now, another plant was just slowly growing.

When we pulled back into the driveway, John's daughter, wearing all black with a blonde B-52 a mile high, stood hips cocked in the driveway.

"She's a hairdresser at the Wal-Mart in Mitchell," he said. "And that's little John," he whispered to me, pointing to the child running in a circle. "We're not sure who Daddy is."

The question mark in his revelation took me aback. I hopped down from the pickup, wiping a wrinkle out of my blazer.

"I'm gonna shoot them," Cynthia said, ". . . the geese . . . You could write that into your story," she said, looking back at me and winking.

From the outside, John's barn looked normal—red paint, low-slung entrance, geese everywhere. But when I looked closer, I saw newer, blonde wood against the older, darker wood.

"When they tore down the dance hall, I salvaged some of the wood," John said.

And I realized I stood inside a whale's skeleton. The dance hall enclosed around me.

"Here are the streamers."

Cynthia's slender hand lifted toward a silver stub hanging from a notch on the wood.

"Do they have dances like this anymore?" I asked.

"Sometimes they've got a DJ or a live band at the bar in Parkston."

"You know, a lot of bands *before* rock n' roll played the Milltown Dance Hall, too," John said. "They say those shows were even more raucous than the rock n' roll bands."

"Who played?" I asked absentmindedly.

His answer felt like a rusty nail lodged into my sneakers.

"Lawrence Welk, you know him?"

"Know the name," I said.

As Cynthia reached to venerate the streamer, I sensed the shuffling of feet on the sawdust floor, the oomph of the drum, the squeeze of the trombone, the shine of the brass, the trickle of melody from the squeezebox, and in the center, the dancers twirling in taffeta.

"Here, touch it," she whispered. "You can almost hear the music."

I needed to get back to town.

I drove down the dirt road, past the woman selling tickets to the corn maze, and departed onto the highway that took me past the ghost town. Goats wading six-inches into the Jim River munched on straw or dirt or cans along the shoreline. Past a sepulcher of trees, shading my gaze from the semicircle sun setting in each of the three rearview mirrors, I felt the landscape transform into super-red barns, golden cornstalks.

Closer to Sioux Falls, I turned the radio to KISD out of Pipestone, Minnesota. Freddie North's "She's All I Got" clamored to me across the prairie into my metallic car. A pink moon rose behind a water tower standing in the middle of nowhere.

Friend, don't take her she's all I got
Please don't take her love away from me!

This was my second reason for the visit to South Dakota on this fall night. At the wedding back in May, I met one of the groom's friends who just returned to living in the Dakotas after a decade in D.C. It was likely one of the last nights to drink outdoors, and when I found Carrie, she was at a patio outside a bar downtown, buttoned up in her coat.

CHAPTER 25

STRASBURG, NORTH DAKOTA

SATURDAY, JUNE 3, 2016

For Carrie's twenty-ninth birthday, I drove her out to Midland, South Dakota, and the Stroeppel Inn, a western-style mineral springs oasis and hotel standing in dry, scrub grass prairie. It's a great place for ornery cattle, skinny buttes, and a rookery of nuclear missiles stored deep underground for an impending nuclear winter.

Sadly, the inn was under new ownership.

"We're up from Georgia," said the woman, cats running around her feet, licking the pizza boxes. "And it's too hot for the baths."

"Oh, really?" I asked, disappointed. We had driven the four hours from Sioux Falls, farther west than I imagined. An hour west of Pierre, even.

"You don't want to soak in that," the woman said, clicking the TV changer. "You'll boil like a lobster."

I don't want to say hospitality is dead anymore. But sometimes you encounter patrons in need of a refresher. Had we stumbled upon Welk's menagerie on a hot day, he would've extended a wide palm from his desk and sat us down to sympathetically explain his dilemma, ideally not opening with water the temperature at which crustaceans cook, and then, instead, produced a squeezebox from the wardrobe and offered to play us a tune or two before sending us out for complimentary steak dinners and returning brusquely to his accounting.

Or maybe not. Regardless, Carrie and I signed the guestbook, spent the night, and got up early the next morning. Grabbing a breakfast of cheese sticks and coffee at the gas station, we headed north to Strasburg.

Just below the border, in Herreid, lawn chairs unpopulated by people sat atop quilts draped along the curb signaling the parade to start later that day. When we reached the business end of North Dakota, a large, green sign stood sentry in the tall grass waving wild and golden green.

"THE LAWRENCE WELK HIGHWAY"

Musical notes dotted the board.

We got out to take a photograph.

Carrie yelled something, but over the whipping wind I couldn't hear.

"What's that?" I held my hand to my ear.

"Smile bigger!"

As it turned out, the state of North Dakota *did* purchase up the Welk estate, and it has operated as a multi-purpose historical site, offering glass-blowing demonstrations along with panels on the Germans from Russia experience.

We actually drove past the road to exit onto the site at least twice before flying down a gravel road and reaching the homestead.

"We're working on getting new signs up," the woman in the house terminating at the gravel's end told us. "Next week, we've got a real blacksmith coming out. Week after, we're hosting a barn dance."

We perused a small gift shop. Carrie picked up a plastic, toy accordion. A bright squeeze of air trickled out as sweet as an apple.

"Maybe for Lila?" she asked, referencing her newborn godchild.

"We can always hope," I replied.

On the tour, our guide pulled back a wooden cutout in the wall so we could see the dried clay bricks insulating the home.

"Better than air conditioning in the summer. Like heating in the winter."

You almost forget you're here to see a celebrity's childhood home, with the sparse kitchen and table, until you enter the living room, with its life-sized cardboard cutout of Welk dressed in a dazzling white suit.

"There he is."

Removing from the house, I spied the pond where Welk bowed to the cows on the night he first crow-barred open a crate containing his European accordion. Staring at the clouds, I could picture a young farm kid, alone, standing on the flat, vast emptiness. It felt much farther away from civilization than Vermillion or Wells.

"It's not just about Welk," cautioned our docent, "But about the Germans from Russia culture, too."

In the barn, Carrie and I stared for a while at the wedding photographs. Pale-faced strangers in black, heavy cloaks absorbed suspiciously by the cameras.

"Lawrence was supposed to have learned entertainment playing three-day weddings," I whispered to Carrie.

"Interesting," she said, eying the grey still-life photographs, with pioneers staring out like inmates trapped in some yellowing stop bath.

Finally, we slouched shoulders to peek into the summer kitchen, where Lawrencell sat on his haunches on the dirt floor, making a rudimentary stringed instrument while Christine and his sisters prepared dinner. As we ducked our heads coming out, Carrie pointed to early retirees, all women, congregating near a car with Wisconsin plates.

"Do you think they came all the way for *this*?"

In one of the more bizarre sections of *Wunnerful, Wunnerful,* Lawrence says he could've been an Olympic swimmer only if his town had a pool. It's a curiously detached musing from his shag carpet, wading in his Palm Springs pool with Quincy Jones and His Orchestra's "Soul Bossa Nova" booming. But we all have regrets at how life may pigtail in other directions.

In town, we spotted a number of structures that, for lack of a better word, felt like antecedents to the pronouns, like the other shoe dropping.

Right away, we hit the newly painted municipal swimming pool. Kids lazily ate ice-cream bars in the lifeguard stations. Some women sunned. In bright black letters on the blue concrete: "Welk Family Pool."

"Maybe he promised it to the town?" I told Carrie.

"It can certainly keep a town together."

Strasburg in many ways resembles a normal, equal parts church and bar town, save a few ostentatious artifacts. A dance club eats up a block downtown. Second, a gazebo with chipped paint sticks up from a grassy yard.

"A Gift from Lawrence Welk," read a sign. The structure looked like it was dropped from space and then halfway grown over with cow pasture.

Driving south, we spotted a green sign announcing Hague, so I took a loping curve on the highway and continued heading due east.

"Where are we going?" Carrie asked.

"The site of Welk's first big show."

Carrie leaned back and put her shades on.

On the morning of his first big show, Welk would've seen that towering steeple of St. Peter and Paul just around that dogleg of a road, like some old-world fortress on the prairie, with his heart beating like a floor tom.

Our red Prius took a fast right into town and pulled up to the church just before Saturday vigil mass, and we slipped through the big, oak doors. According to a history pamphlet stuffed into the antechamber, the original church burnt in a fire. What now stands—what we stood in—was an exact replica.

We peeked inside the ornate chapel, spying the German wood-carving chancel rail. A beautiful, plump organ set in the middle. I tried to imagine young Lawrence, kneeling, trembling, holding the blood of Christ, taking the Eucharist before returning to his pew, his armpits sweating madly with nerves, before sprinting out into that August morning and down the street to sell tickets.

"I admire his courage," I whispered to Carrie. "Do you know how hard it is getting up for mass after playing a Saturday night show?"

Downtown, we found a café and that car with Wisconsin plates sitting outside on the otherwise-empty street. We walked in and saw the women eating pie in the corner. A sixteen-year-old waitress took orders behind a glass counter. "Two lemonades and some blueberry pie," Carrie said.

Journalist or no journalist, I felt like now was the time to track this all down. "Say," I interjected, "Do you know where the old opera house is?"

The sixteen-year-old girl cocked her eyebrow. "There's no opera . . . thing," she said.

"Oh," I said. "Well, it's just in this book, there was once an opera house, here in Hague. Or *The* Hague, North Dakota."

"Hold up," the girl said, walking over to an open doorway in back. Then she hollered. "Mom!" A woman with a braid and a wide, serious face emerged from the back room. "Yes?"

"This guy's got a question."

I felt things had progressed far too much.

"Can I help you?" she asked, sternly. She had taken the approach of someone ready to send back a retort about their lack of gluten-free options. But my request was far more asinine.

"Did you ever have an opera house in town?"

She answered squarely. "We never had one," she said. "No opera house in this town." I nodded, smiling at her clarification, and went to sit down. "We'll have your pie out in a second."

Carrie was already talking to the women near us. "No," they said. "We just thought we'd make a girls' weekend of it." "We just always loved his show," assured another woman. "When we heard this place was open, we wanted to come over and check it out."

Quiet is how I often became around the real Welk fans, who earnestly and without any latter-day thesis stored on their laptop pay respects to their star. I don't think that Welk is an artifact of some lost utopia on the prairie, some time in America when morality mattered, and I don't think that common decency is buried on a series of VHS cassette tapes in Grandpa's barn.

But no one's ever told me this straightaway either. They usually just tell me they liked his music. Or as a writer who grew up in a Black neighborhood in south Minneapolis once explained it to me: "Why'd we watch him?" she laughed. "Because he was the only music on TV."

The parade in Herreid was finished when we drove back into South Dakota—folding chairs and quilts gone, a street dance beginning to mobilize over by a beer garden.

Carrie watched out the window, green soybeans molting copper coats. East of Aberdeen, coming back into civilization, we picked up more radio stations. As the sun gently folded behind the western plains, we found a public radio station, just as that Duluth old-timey guitarist Charlie Parr's recording of "Ain't No Grave" carried over the flat horizon on public radio.

Ain't no grave—gonna hold my body down.
Hear that trumpet sound—better get up off the ground.
Ain't no grave—gonna hold my body down.

And I felt that bite—that all musicians feel—when someone's working, while you're sitting in the crowd.

CHAPTER 26

THE IMPERIAL BALLROOM, RAPID CITY, SOUTH DAKOTA

MONDAY, OCTOBER 5, 2007

The Brickhouse Boys hit the road again in the indefatigable, ozone-depleting S.S. *Robert Bly* that fall. After Bobby got "Waterloo" in his inbox, he called me up on a Friday night, a few nights after the Throwback opened up for Thrice, and I met him on his leaf-strewn stoop. He wore a black leather jacket and svelte brown Chelsea boots and appeared reconciliatory.

"How'd the show go?" I asked.

"Could do a hundred shows like that and wouldn't be the same as Brick, man," he said. "Hey, did you hear Pie-eater broke up?"

I had heard rumblings. Days earlier, one morning before class, I'd run into Donny and Monster smoking a cigarette outside Old Main on campus. It was the same day Radiohead released *In Rainbows* for free over the Internet, so the two were discussing the new tracks. I needed to go teach, but Donny grabbed me and warned me that his Pie-eater bandmate, Virgil, had been ornery about us using the *Bly* on tour that summer.

"Ahh, that's too bad," I told Bobby.

"Nah, drummer's got to know his role," said Bobby. "He doesn't need to get you worked up about that. Just keep on the lookout."[1]

"You get a chance to listen to that song I sent you?"

"Waterloo?" asked Bobby. "It's brilliant, man."

He pulled out his phone and played a vocal recording he'd laid down.

"Nice," I said. "I like how it veers from the, you know, piano lick."

We walked down to Maya Jane's bar in Vermillion, lights flickering on the streetlamps, and sat at one of the booths, planning our next batch of shows. We'd throw away the uniforms. We'd practice more. But we also didn't talk about band stuff at all. It felt like our time before the band. Until Poncho, who'd moved down to Vermillion to cook at the bar, popped his head out of the kitchen.

"I got some friends in this band out in California who could record that song for us," he yelled. "The band Fishbone! You in?"

And our fall calendar was inked.

After the Corn Palace, our rocket ship shot higher into the regional stratosphere, landing gigs in Sioux City, Madison, Sioux Falls. We went back up to Minneapolis to play the 400 Bar, this time taking two vehicles so I could catch up on reading. On that next night, a Saturday, we arrived late to our gig in Brookings. An early winter wind blew under an orange moon. It was homecoming down in Vermillion, so the Brookings streets felt desolate. Just after we cleared the gear from the van and sound-checked, Monster ran in screaming to the whole Safari Lounge, from the Big Buck Hunter console to the door.

"Someone stole the *Bly*!"

Heads from the bar turned in alarm. Donny called 911. Then he and his brother borrowed my car keys and took off toward the interstate. Everyone knew it was Virgil. But they couldn't find him.

So we played our show anyway.

"We've got merch in back," Poncho announced.

"Also, someone stole our van," added Leo.

The free publicity was magnificent. People poured into the bar

---

1. A week later, I was startled on a walk back from campus when the S.S. *Bly* blew past me on a side street, kicking up yellow leaves, with Monster and Bobby in the front seat. "We're going to park this where Virgil will never find it!" they shouted, careening down Forest Avenue.

in their stocking caps and flannel just to look at us. Sure, we'd lost the van (though only for the night—fortunately, Donny had locked the "Club" to the steering wheel, so apparently Virgil just drove the thing straight, taking no turns, and abandoned ship four blocks away, where the police found the *Bly* the next day). But the guys got a ride back to Sioux Falls from a friend. Also, yes, we had to cancel a Sunday gig in Lincoln. But the heist actually supplanted our band's meager standing in the public eye. Our MySpace plays skyrocketed that night. We even made local TV news.

Two nights later, on Monday, we traversed the state to open up for a touring act, a synthpop group called Shiny Toy Guns, at Rapid City's Imperial Ballroom. That band would be nominated for a Grammy in a few months, and our set was Beatles-play-Shea-Stadium wild. Before Bobby even sang a word, the kids, like hundreds, started screaming, crying out for us. One girl just lunged for Leo's pant-leg. Afterward, we huddled around the bus. Security roped us off. When the lead singer emerged, smoky-eyed, Poncho stuck out a poster to sign like a fan who'd won an FM radio call-in contest.

"We, we, we opened for you," Poncho said.

"I didn't even know there was an opening band," she said. "Otherwise, I would've come seen you."

She gracefully floated away from the droning bus with blinds pulled down, her legs wrapped in black, skintight denim. According to her Wikipedia (that I later read), we were the same age. But any envy I had that night would soon be buried when STG knocked out the power at the old hotel—twice—sending the ensemble scampering back onto the bus. Howling with laughter, my brother and I would fly off into the night, heading eastward in my purple, '98 Cavalier, cutting across the Badlands with Leo driving and me writing a graduate essay on Hayden White's ideas about historiographic metafiction, the car's dash light illuminating my laptop.

The energy felt good. Two weeks later, we headlined a zombie pub crawl at an Irish pub in Sioux Falls. A drunken Angus showed up and sprayed fake blood on my keyboard, but I passed the night sitting at the bar reading Marx's *Das Kapital* for class. I really felt I was getting the hang of things. Word came in, as well, that over Thanksgiving we would definitely tour with the veteran California ska/punk band, Fishbone. Talk had even spread of a television special.

"It'll be on South Dakota Public Broadcasting," Bobby said. "Statewide."

Sure, balancing my grad studies with the band was a dilemma. But I felt the frantic pace was necessary. Welk says in his book that he pushed the band through a blizzard to reach a gig in Salt Lake City. Sure, he left the drummer bandaged with frostbite on his hands, but he made the gig.

On another night that frenzied fall, Collette and I ate pumpkin pie from a plastic tin on a bench outside the new Wal-Mart. Its tall, *War of the Worlds*-style floodlights washed brown across the sable sky.

"How many weekends in a row have you missed?"

"Too many."

She had insisted on taking a break after spotting me pacing the lounge at the Newman Center around midnight so that I wouldn't fall asleep reading *Moby-Dick*.

My body ached. I had red rings around my eyes.

A few days later, Dr. Hader sat me down.

"You're going to need to decide if you want to keep doing your band or not," she told me, understandingly. "You could go on and get your doctorate."

I hedged my bets, hoping one thing—school or the band—would break. My brother wearied, too. A couple times he cried in the car riding to gigs, just broken down, sniffling in the passenger seat, but I sensed we could break through with the right audience—a limousine errantly traveling through the Dakotas or a guy whose sister's boyfriend works in New York City. I sensed the right tie was all we needed.

By early November, gearing up for a big fundraiser gig for the English department in Vermillion, I got a midday call on Wednesday from Mom. I figured it was either an accidental dial or someone had died.

"Grandma just passed away," she said. "The wake will be on a Friday. Just thought I'd let you know."

"But we have a show Friday night!"

"Tough."

CHAPTER 27

VERDIGRE, NEBRASKA

FRIDAY, NOVEMBER 11, 2007

There's a moment in the biopic when the artist decides how to respond to the call of life.

In *The Red Shoes*, the backstage drama about an obsessive ballerina, Vicki (who answers Lermontov's question of "why do you dance?" with "why do you live?") runs off with Craster rather than remaining subservient to her tyrannical Svengali.

In *The Jazz Singer*, a nobody-to-star metamorphosis filmed in the very studio that housed tapings of *The Lawrence Welk Show*, Jack Rubin forgoes his Broadway debut to sing in his father's stead for Yom Kippur, costing him his fame.

Even in *Babette's Feast*, a film my mother rented for us as children, we see the gift unused when the great French chef toils away in service to her Danish patrons who provided her shelter after she lost everything.

The artist, the art, and the life are entwined. To sever one, for whatever temporary gain, means losing them all in the end.

But it all depends on your interpretation, I suppose. Each film is about the sacrifice artists make to live life. But the artist finds a way, nonetheless, in winnowing moments of capacity and possibility, to create.

Virginia Vondracek had suffered memory loss for years and slept one night without getting up. I immediately contemplated canceling our Friday night show.

"I bet you could skip out during Friday's wake," Dad said.

Transportation realities—like pocket-sized etiquette books—always help navigate the cloudy waters of grief. This was something I knew from Welk's books.

Back in the mid-1930s when Welk was high on the hog in St. Paul, fishing on executive lakes, playing for the ritzy clans named in Fitzgerald's novels, he received melancholy word that his father had passed from uremic poisoning.

He got in his car, pointed toward the flatlands of North Dakota. But "the roads became so slick and icy my car skidded wildly and turned over and over, landing in a ditch at the side of the road. I was not hurt, just dazed and shaken, but the car was almost demolished."

Lawrence never made it to Ludwig's funeral.

Friday afternoon, Leo and I zipped down the river road south of Yankton along the Missouri, through the Santee Sioux reservation, and eventually into the bluffs running along the Verdigre Creek. My brother talked speedily about Bret Michaels from Poison.

"But do you think he knows how to play a 7th chord, that's what I'm asking?"

Around 5 p.m., we pulled up to the funeral home in Verdigre. Shiny SUVs lined the muddy parking lot. Cousins, aunts, uncles, and neighbors from town filed into the building. We signed the guestbook and greeted our relatives, when a dilatory rental car arrived.

"That must be Mike," said Dad.

"It's him," Leo whispered.

Out stepped a man with blue eyes and a salt-n-pepper beard, a ponytail pulled back. He wore a black suit. Uncle Mike was in the Nebraska Rock n' Roll Hall of Fame.

When Lawrence and the band matriculated to Pittsburgh, a few years after his father passed away, he received another telegram.

"Come home at once. Mother is dying."

Lawrence approached the manager of the Kennywood Amusement Park, who felt so moved by the wishes of a bereaved son that he found a hole in his calendar just big enough for one day. "You can fly in and see her and probably be back for the show tomorrow night," he said.

A thick fog off the Ohio River grounded planes, however. Lawrence rushed back to his hotel room to place a call. "Mother just slept away very peacefully . . . We were all here," said a brother.

"Christopher, Leo!" Mike called, firmly grabbing our hands. "I heard you guys got a gig tonight. I wish I could make it, but under the circumstances . . ."

Uncle Mike fronted the Sound of Fate and toured the Midwest and East Coast. They had done a summer in Estes Park, won the 1970 Nebraska State Fair competition, and run to Florida, where Mike landed a gig at Disney World, before running an arts elementary school in Orlando.

"George sent your music. Love it. Rich piano, gritty sound. That a real piano isn't it?"

"A Fazioli."

"I was gonna guess. Doesn't have the high ting of a Yamaha or one of the Japanese models. But I dig it."

Mike's voice had the crackling, limitless coolness of vintage musicians in biopic interviews, perpetually gesticulated with a lit cigarette.

Leo jumped in, "We're playing the Eagles Club in Vermillion. You ever do there?"

"With the Fate?" Mike asked.

Ahhh, the Fate. Like Chili Peppers or Floyd, the Fate carried the reverence of brevity.

"Mike," our Dad called. "What was that story about the Fate over in Niobrara?" Leo and I were surprised to see our dad talking rock n' roll.

Mike straightened his black tie and lingered for a moment in the foray. "They didn't provide us any monitors up the river in Niobrara. So, we just figured we'd turn it up. And then when we couldn't hear anything, we turned up more." He gestured like rain from the sky. "Plaster started coming off the ceiling."

It could've been a Brickhouse story.

Standing beside my aunts in the lobby, I felt sheepish running to Vermillion to play a gig. "Don't worry, Christopher," said my dad's eldest sister, Jennifer. "Grandma loved hearing you play." "Plus," said my dad's youngest sister, Laurie, "You never know what's to blame for the crib."

"What crib?"

"You know about the crib, don't you, Christopher? Rita!" Jennifer called in a loud whisper to my mom, wearing a black dress. "You've told the boys about the crib, right?"

Mom shook her face intensely, her black hair framing her expression of oversight. "I thought we had, but maybe not. George?"

She nudged Dad, chatting with an old teacher. He raised his hand up to say *don't bother me right now*.

"It's an old family legend about this crib that came over from Europe with grandpa's grandfather. He was a musician, and the story was if you slept in that crib as a child, you would grow up to be a musician."

My brother, standing next to me, turned around.

"What in the . . . ?"

"Most the grandkids were raised in the crib," said Laurie. "Except Ian," said Meghan.

Ian, her brother, shrugged his shoulders. The facts were evident, I just had never taken the time to see what was so obviously before me. Meghan was a band director, just like her father, like her grandfather, like her uncles, including my father. She played the trombone. My dad played tuba. Uncle Tom played trumpet. Grandpa played tuba. Laurie played flute. Jennifer played the flute and directed choir. Uncle Mike played piano and trumpet. Cousin Zach played viola. Cousin Victor, the drums. Cousin Ellie, the clarinet. Cousin Addie on the bassoon. Cousin Ethan played the tuba. Cousin Amanda, the trumpet. Leo played clarinet. I was percussion and piano. Shaking the priest's hand was my dad's cousin, David. He directed the band in Verdigre. Their whole family played instruments, too.

How had this never been consciously apparent to me? Somehow, I let the noun "musician" be squeezed too narrowly, excluding the hobbyists, the part-timers, the teachers, the reputable, the diligent, the impassioned locals.

"Was I raised in it?" I asked, turning to Mom. "The crib?"

"I know Leo was," Dad smiled.

"*But what about me?*"

"Oh of course you were, geez Louise," Mom said. "You both were. You both are talented musicians."

She used her teacher's voice.

CHAPTER 28

BASEMENT OF ST. WENCESLAUS CHURCH IN VERDIGRE, NEBRASKA

NOVEMBER 9, 2007

When Lawrence Welk and His Champagne Orchestra arrived at the Aragon Ballroom at the north end of Venice Beach, he was on a roll. He had traveled the country as Miller Lite's house band and played the nation's finest venues, including Pops Sadrup's oceanside ballroom.

In 1946, he wrote the joint "looked just like a big barn!"

On Lick Pier in Santa Monica, the Aragon was nestled near shooting galleries and games of chance on a boardwalk and was within the shadow of a double Ferris wheel and carousel that lit up the night sky.

Close to the ocean, Welk feared the structure might rush out to sea, trombones dunked in the surf.

But when Welk returned in 1951, colorful paint stripped off in dreary slabs. The carnival on the boardwalk slowed to an oscillating twitch, like a vinyl record unplugged. Busted beer bottles and trash lined the street.

"What in the world happened?" Lawrence asked Pops.

"Ah well, you know. The ballroom business has just gone to pot."

But Welk—like he did with the Chevrolet dealer in Aberdeen—had an idea. He had scheduled a broadcast over KTLA and wanted to use a refurbished Aragon Ballroom.

They tidied up the old bird, strung up new lights, repaired busted windows. And on a Friday night, they went live all across southern California.

It was just like the old days.

Big cars drove up from Huntington and Manhattan Beach weekly. When Lawrence won over the stable of southern California Dodge dealers, his show stayed on four years. It's all fine and good. But that's not the part I love.

A moment in *Wunnerful, Wunnerful* remains difficult to fit into the larger puzzle.

After some pleading with Fern, she moved the family—for the last time—out to Los Angeles, and for four years, *The Lawrence Welk Show* was broadcast weekly on KTLA out of Los Angeles. Ratings were strong, and in 1955, Lawrence received word that ABC would like to put *The Lawrence Welk Show* on nationally for summer sweeps.

The planners scheduled a meeting at the Aragon. Lawrence arrived early, set up folding chairs, and poured coffee. Sales directors and agency heads greeted him, as he removed a typed-out setlist of the first show.

"Here it is!"

John Gaunt, the ad man, took it from Welk's hands and ripped it up.

"Lawrence's music may be all right with the Okies or the folks back home in North Dakota," he said, "But it will never hold up with a nationwide audience."

The table erupted, suggesting a comedian, some "big production numbers," maybe a "line of girls."

Lawrence wanted to hurl himself overboard. Within a few short pen-strokes, the group threatened to trash his show, and before Welk realized what he was doing, he stood up.

"Gentlemen," he clutched his list of songs. "Just a moment please! I want to do this show more than I can say. But, I'll give it up, before I'll do it this way!"

All Lawrence heard was the countless bar managers, promoters, and other small-time tycoons who tried telling him what *won't* sell on the coasts, or in Pittsburgh, L.A., Chicago, or in Dallas, and how time after time he, the North Dakotan with the accordion, had the better instincts.

"Gentlemen, may I explain what's in my heart?"

In the church basement, after the funeral and luncheon, I spotted Grandpa sitting alone in his chair. The blue pant legs of his suit hiked mid-way up his calf, revealing his orthopedic socks.

"Your dad says you're writing about Lawrence Welk?"

"I'm thinking about it," I said. "Did you know him?"

Grandpa smiled, revealing a missing tooth. "I never played with Welk," he said, folding his large, round hands, "But I played with people he played with. Welk says the unions chased him out because they didn't want the competition. Baloney." Grandpa waved his hands. "Welk was a cheapskate."

Uncle Mike walked over and pulled out a chair.

"He paid his musicians scale."

"What's this story about Opal?" I asked. "The lounge singer from Sioux City."

Grandpa stroked his mostly-salt beard. "Opal, Virginia's brother, Lawrence's friend, used to sing in lounges down in Sioux City. Grandma loved her voice. Opal used to gig with Welk, too . . . Lincoln, Omaha. She was a good singer. But Welk paid her *well beneath* other singers."

"Years later," Grandpa continued, sipping from his Styrofoam cup, "Welk came to Omaha, and Opal hung out in the lobby of the hotel they were staying at. She figured out his room and early in the morning knocked on his door. Welk answers, and she looks and says, 'Welk you can rot in hell.' Then she delivers him breakfast and walks away."

A staccato of laughter roiled the crowd that had scattered across folding chairs on the tiled basement floor. Uncles and cousins and aunts enjoyed hearing the story again.

"Some say *cheap*," said Aunt Kathy, defending Welk. "I'd just call him *frugal*."

"Say what you will," Mike said, "He made it. A lot of guys don't."

"He hired local," my dad said.

"Not just because they were local," Grandpa said. "They used to have some good players around."

The words, Lawrence says, formed before him.

In television, they need to worry about the mothers that will turn off the show if a comedian goes blue, or that if a trumpet player falls in love with a dancing girl it will impact his playing.

As Lawrence explained, if the mother "feels something is not quite right—she will just get up and turn the program right off. You have lost her—and may I say, she's not very apt to go out and buy a Dodge car, either!"

Then he sat down to a boardroom filled with applause.

Well, in the movie version. Actually, the board still wasn't convinced. It took the mellifluous tongue of the Dodge guy to convince everyone Welk should be allowed to run his own show.

But even if his speech tacked unfair to dancers or comedians, his fidelity to his music counted with me. An artist? A musician? An entertainer? I'm not one for tight distinctions.

When I asked Mom why Welk was so economical, she said, "I grew up with people like his family. The *only* way he could've done that as a career was if he treated it as a trade."

Leo and I drove back to Vermillion in the afternoon.

"Doesn't that thought of Grandma working all the time make you feel guilty?" I asked. "Like, she worked, so we could do what? Go to graduate school? Screw around in this band?"

"Maybe it's what they wanted, though," Leo said. "For us to have opportunities they didn't."

We drove past a couple of bent-over women cutouts. Dead leaves filled the gutters. Everyone watched the Cornhuskers. Bells clanged, echoing across silent streetscapes if the team scored a touchdown.

We drove in silence.

"Funerals scare me," Leo said.

The road took us first up the hillside overlooking Verdigre Creek into Niobrara, situated on a hillside to avoid the backwater caused when the Corps of Engineers built the dam in the wrong spot. A long bridge spans the divide.

At the gas station, we bought Mello Yellos. The seclusion of small, Midwestern towns used to comfort me. Particularly when they see me coming from somewhere else. In that brief exchange of a credit card, a nonplussed glance, the cashier might think you're anyone dressed up in a suit, long hair, sunglasses. In these towns, you can be someone. The trick is to not hang around too long to let them find out otherwise.

"Where have I seen you guys before?" the cashier asked.

"We're in a band," Leo said.

She smiled and handed us our change for our roasted peanuts and orange pop. She only half understood.

"On behalf of all of us, I want to thank you for choosing to shop at our little store."

We met her smile with bigger smiles and exited, pretending to be in a hurry.

CHAPTER 29

OUR CARRIAGE HOUSE IN
WASHINGTON, D.C.

TUESDAY, JULY 16, 2019

In the fourth paragraph of his book, Welk writes, "Sounds always fascinated me." Then he launches into a screed filled with melodic nouns, "sod farmhouse," "accordion," "pearl buttons."

The conversation around music is what fascinates me. Writing *about* music. It's a shame this book carries no melody, no sound of the things I talk of, but I hope there is an echo. And not just of the *tinkling* piano or the *blaring* horns but of the backfiring pickup and inelegant bullfrog, *ribbit-ribbit-ribbit-ing* on the marsh in the bluestem ditch.

When I look back on my writing, I keep seeing this phrase, *oom-pa-pa*. I found it an essay I wrote my senior year.

I convinced a van full of friends to drive to the CBS studios in North Mankato, overlooking the Minnesota River, and dance for an hour on a taping of *Bandwagon*. When my teacher retired, she passed on my essay to my dad, still the band director at the high school.

"The white lights begin to sizzle now," the essay opens. "High above, strung up like carcasses of meat, the lights bake down on the crowd and the band."

I'd gotten carried away.

"Before Eminem, there was Elvis, and before Elvis, there were the Chimeleski Brothers."

What was I talking about?

I even quoted someone named "Gene," who told me, "Not even *Gunsmoke* has been on as long as us."

But toward the end is the line: "As the jolly tuba *oom-pa-pas* away with the first notes of 'Suzy Polka,' the resurrected dancers spring back to life."

Bandwagon had broadcast from the KEYC studios for forty-three years by 2003. The polka variety show took marching orders from *The Lawrence Welk Show*, drawing from the lace dirndl-and-pheasant-hatted romper crowd from New Ulm and a couple of caravans from a community caring for people with intellectual disabilities. My friends and I went three times, before an older man with suspenders and yellow pit stains continued to force me to play the backstage piano, sitting near me, whispering to "keep playing the pedals, the pedals," which was just a harmless tick but nevertheless kept me away.

Still, I'll never forget the new-leaf-blower-on-Father's-Day look of surprise on the face of the hosts when a bunch of kids first showed up on a cold autumn night into the warm television ballroom. And we started a tradition. For years, kids from my school kept going up to the studios.

Anyway, my last paragraph ends like so: "Extending its right foot in a box-step and its left hand around one's back, *Bandwagon* jumps out of the screen on that first note and carries you off into the distance, escaping under the moon, defying the cynics. Song and dance. That is all *Bandwagon* is. Song and dance, that is all anyone needs."

The paper got a B.

Mrs. Jane Johnson taught with my mother for years in Iowa. When I was a child, Mom stuffed me into a parka in that Chevette, drove in and set me up in the teacher's lounge on snow days. Mrs. Johnson remembered me and assumed I inherited my mom's appreciation for language. But she was a good writing teacher.

She wrote: "Chris: the intro feels a bit heavy. As do a few other places. Sometimes <u>less</u> (wording) is <u>more</u>."

In college, the phrase would come to find me again.

The summer before my senior year, I got an internship at the *West Central Tribune* in Willmar, Minnesota. My reporting chops weren't strong. I had to Wikipedia "water main" before talking to the water superintendent. So perhaps sensing the stripes of this intern, my editor asked if I wanted a feature story. I could brainstorm it all on my own, he said. I immediately knew.

The first Wednesday in town, I went for a run but turned around mid-step after hearing the trains of a brass band in the park. Maybe a hundred people sat in folding chairs with visors on, *Uff Da* cups at their feet, sunglasses on, watching, listening. The band played the hits—Sousa, Rachmaninoff, and Barber. Maybe it was something lighter, showtunes or Disney. Regardless, I felt lifted, transported.

The next Wednesday, I showed up to a rehearsal. I sat in back and took notes. When the concert started, children danced, old people tapped feet, a solitary man stood near trees, watching safely from afar. I stayed around to chat with the director afterward.

"See you next week?" he asked.

I was confused.

"We figured we should ask you to join us?"

It was the band's final performance before the Fourth of July. That night, I ran back to the newsroom, still with the 10 p.m. deadline approaching, and typed out a story.

Writing about music is always homage, a proxy.

Sitting at my desk at the *West Central Tribune,* I struggled for a moment with the attention-getter, and then it hit me.

"If you're out for a walk on a Wednesday night and think you hear the sound of a tuba's oom-pa-pa wafting toward you from the park, you're not hearing things."

The phrase flew to me like a bird, scraggly and spontaneous from somewhere in the darkened eaves of my memory: *oom-pa-pa.* My editors loved it. I thought it was serviceable.

The next Wednesday, I showed up to the park at the same time, and learned the sheet music (Barnum & Bailey's), and then came showtime. As we played, I watched for her to arrive. She told me she would leave Vermillion after finishing her summer class. During our final song, I looked up and saw Heather, in denim capris and a white sleeveless shirt, strolling up. She had done her hair and smelled like lavender. When we kissed, I felt like I belonged to an order of people, a line, a strand of the populace, with one foot in the arts and one foot in life, loving and living at the same time.

But I was mistaken.

I had a longer journey to go still. I hesitate to say I was an artist, or a writer, or an onomatopoet. But I still shuffled along, needing a project, and looking back on that person in Willmar is like visiting a ghost of myself, someone who was present, but not yet fully awake.

Oom-pa-pa is still the onomatopoeia I prefer. More than *buzz, slap, howl,* or *clatter, oom-pa-pa* is closer to the feel of the dance than most words.

"Onomatopoeia" in English means "imitating sound." I like this definition in terms of *The Lawrence Welk Show,* which was imitation as music—imitating a bandstand, imitating a dance night, imitating a butterfly. Picasso said all art in some way imitates if only to reveal the truth.[1]

Lawrence Welk opened each show popping a finger in his mouth, imitating the miniature explosion of a champagne cork. But in Greek, "onomatopoeia," is understood not as imitation, but as "making a name."

The wind blew.

The grass rustled.

The cicadas *see-saaawed.*

For years, I wished I kept my other name: Éamon.

When I was born, Mom named me for the Gaelic version of

---

1. But even that came in an Orson Welles film about fakery, so I'm not sure there, either.

"Edmund." Dad went to school and told everyone his son's name: Éamon. In the Albert Lea hospital, however, a nun visited my mother.

"I've always loved the name Christopher," she said. "The patron saint of travelers."

Mom, devoutly Catholic, made the switch.

Christopher, according to the Church before the 1960s, apparently ferried travelers across the waters and once gave a lift to a child who grew to be Christ. I don't know if there is a patron saint of traveling musicians. I doubt it. But I think one travels with stories.

When I began writing this story with Welk, I only carried something small, perhaps a biography of a bizarre musician who stumbled upon me. In the many years since, I've realized Welk wasn't carrying me, but I carried myself, or stories of my family, on my back, standing over the water, the Jim, the Missouri, the Verdigris, safely into the small towns of people now swallowed on the prairie into silent graves.

The thing about my second-grade recital piece, "Oom Pa Pa," that I sometimes overlook is that I stayed with it. Each year, I came back for the recital. Each time, I remembered that first one. I never made a mistake like that again.

By my senior year, I performed—admittedly a slightly truncated version—Gershwin's "Rhapsody in Blue." And Mrs. Carlson smiled proudly, perhaps in relief, from behind the podium, now a little older, her bright eyes and puffy hair and tasteful red suit coat still her own.

The night of "Oom Pa Pa," I wanted to go back because it's human to want to go back and fix something that you've done wrong, that you know you could've done right. Like a relationship, a band, a book. It's where music comes from—to forget, to paper over, and to remember in a different way, or as exactly as it was, had you only been fully paying attention.

CHAPTER 30

LU ELLA'S APARTMENT IN YANKTON, SOUTH DAKOTA

TUESDAY, AUGUST 11, 2016

The meeting with Lu Ella had been in motion for almost weeks. Carrie's father—a hip and knee surgeon in Yankton—told me his patients knew Lawrence Welk. So shortly thereafter, I was on the phone with Lu Ella setting up this interview.

After *Polka Go Round* ended, Lou and Lu Ella went back on the road with their children, who sang in harmony. They flew a propjet to gigs.

Lu Ella handed me a photograph of her husband next to the Cessna. "Lou 'Flying Fingers' Prohut" read the orange letters. In the creased image, Lou wore a fedora, his accordion draped like a turtle shell around his front side. He was ruddy with a chiseled jawbone.

"Oh, very handsome," Carrie said, warmly.

"The night Lew played Lawrence's show, I actually looked down in the control room of the studio and saw I wore mismatched pumps—one blue and one black," Lu Ella said.

Finally, we got down to brass tacks.

"When did you first see him?" Carrie asked.

"On December 7, 1941."

A big black banner hung in the Sioux City Auditorium announcing "Lawrence Welk and His Champagne Music Makers." Lu Ella, just a girl, had come with her father down from Yankton. Before the show started, the scrim dropped, a newsreel played.

"It was just terrible," she said. "The planes, the crashing, the people's cries. No one had even heard of 'Pearl Harbor.'"

Lu Ella took a sip of water.

"My dad just sat there so still," Lu Ella said. "But here's the thing I'll never forget. I looked up, and there he was between the curtains."

The maestro had his hand to his ear.

"It took me a few seconds to realize what he was doing," Lu Ella said. "He was testing for acoustics."

"Why didn't he stop?" Carrie asked, her inner patriotism triggered.

"You should know the answer, Christopher," Lu Ella said, looking to me.

I paused for a moment before the phrase came to me.

"The show must go on," I said.

"That's the only rule, isn't it?"

Grey drops of rain pelting the windows eased up. Lu Ella poured Carrie and me lemonade and asked if we were cheering for the U.S. Olympics team that night in swimming, the cicadas buzzing outside. After a small side chat, I looked at the clock. Our time ran low.

"There's just one more thing, Lu Ella," I said, pivoting.

"Yes?"

I sensed the door closing on my opportunity.

"Do you know if Lawrence had, you know, like . . . another woman?"

Lu Ella blinked slowly, like I'd asked her where bighorn sheep could open up a checking account in town.

"You know . . . on the side?" I qualified.

Lu Ella was a social firecracker back in her day, the kind of woman musicians punched each other out in alleyways over.

"Christopher," she said with my full three syllables. "You're barking up the wrong tree there."

"Why's that?"

She stared at me calmly, searching for an answer that wouldn't miss slicing the issue exactly as it needed to be sliced.

"He wouldn't have had the time."

There are a million band-director jokes about time.

Q: How can you tell a drummer is at the door?

A: The knocking speeds up.

That kind of thing, ad nauseam.

Musicians, especially conductors, will tell you time is irrelevant. 3/4, 4/4, 6/8, 12/8. Their hand moves the same. What matters is tempo. What matters is beat. Time is just how you *keep* the beat. Hold it. Frame it. Talk about it. Sometimes music has no time at all. But beat, what you do with time, how you talk about time, how you shape it, is everything.

And sometimes, time—and the music—can stop.

When we walked out, Carrie asked me, "Do you have everything you need?"

The clouds chased over the purple parking lot, leaving deep blue pools.

"I think so."

She popped open her pink umbrella. We walked quietly to the car and got onto the road, with its purple, quartzite stones they used as pavement for generations.

"Well, get writing."

CHAPTER 31

STUDIOS OF SOUTH DAKOTA PUBLIC BROADCASTING, VERMILLION

MONDAY, DECEMBER 3, 2007

In December, the Brickhouse Boys were asked onto television because some cameraman at SDPB recruited us to play the reboot of an *Austin City Limits*-style show called *No Cover, No Minimum*. They got A-list South Dakota bands such as Brule, a Native-rock band, and Snakebeard Jackson, a bluegrass crew.

And then, surprisingly, us.

Ever since climbing on stage and dropping his pants at his friend Angus's birthday at the Wessington Springs Opera Hall last June, that cameraman had been blowing absolute roses about this band he shared the stage with called the Brickhouse Boys.

Lawrence got the boot from ABC long before he'd known what was what.

The FCC demanded networks return a half hour to local programming, a move that shuffled the primetime lineups.

"By March, tensions were running very high," Lawrence admits, as his show was bumped to 7:30 from 8:30, a slot he'd held for sixteen years.

But the show "was better than ever." Still, ABC wanted to skew younger. Welk tried performing rock n' roll numbers, from the Beatles to Burt Bacharach. He even had a remake of "One Toke Over the Line," which Lawrence mistakenly thought was gospel.

But the ratings didn't bump.

Our day was long. Tension between us had grown. On Black Friday, we played a full house at Nutty's North in Sioux Falls, opening up for Fishbone. That next morning, we recorded "Waterloo" with Angelo Moore, Fishbone's leader, laying down a spoken word track and saxophones in a studio near the train tracks in Sioux Falls. That Saturday night, up in Moorhead, the Gen Xers who showed up hated us. It was a weird venue, too. The stage was lofted above the bar. All night, animosity grew during our set. So Bobby turned to me.

"I'm going to jump."

"No!"

During our final song, Bobby leapt from the stage about ten feet, landing feet up on the bar, and then somersaulting onto the floor and running out the door. The bartender was livid. But Fishbone's drummer marveled. Only later, after we'd driven home (we now traveled separately from the van), did I find out that Fishbone's drummer was so impressed he wanted to sign us to his label called, well, something lewd that I'll just refer to here as Robert Bly Records.

I couldn't join a label with a name I couldn't share with my grandma. This wasn't a rule. But I was fine making it my own.

Monday afternoon in the studios of South Dakota Public Broadcasting, Bobby and I sat for an interview with the producers.

Q: How did the band form?

Me: We worked for the student newspaper.

Q: How do you come up with songs?

Me: I sit at a piano, banging out chords and then . . .

Bobby: The band writes them. No one gets sole credit.

Q: Where does the name come from?

Bobby: It's a botched reference to David Lynch but . . .

Before the gig, Donny gathered us together. "We're going in there and destroying the place, okay?"

I walked onstage in front of the one-hundred-plus studio audience. On my stool, I waited for the camera's red light. The studio was the same one used a few times a year when the station held a telethon to raise money in front of giant posters featuring characters from popular television shows, like Big Bird, Irish tenor Danny O'Donnell, and Lawrence Welk, grinning and holding a baton.

The countdown started: "three, two, one . . ." The red light blinked on. The show began.

On Tuesday, March 12, 1971, Welk's heart stopped when he read in trade papers his show was "probably going to be dropped." His bosses told him: *wait a week.*

By Friday, with no news from New York, Larry took in golf down in Escondido. He finished the fourteenth hole "at par." Then a "messenger" approached.

Welk was hesitant. He had four more holes to go. "But it's long distance," the messenger said. So he went to the clubhouse to await the return call.

"Hello?"

"Mr. Welk?"

"Yes, speaking."

"This is Rick Du Brow of UPI . . . Mr. Welk, ABC has just released its official list of shows for the new fall season. Your show is not on the list. How do you feel about that?"

Lawrence was clobbered. Then, politely, he picked himself up, reflected, and with utmost grace and clarity, responded.

Collette and I sat at a Mexican restaurant after the gig.

"You know I've been thinking, and of course Heather could've dated a musician. She just didn't want to date *me*."

"I could've told you that," Collette said. "Say, are you going to be mad if I say something?"

"Go ahead."

"I didn't like the show that much."

I nearly spit out my beer.

"What?!"

"The sound is so dark and mean. What's Bobby even *saying*?"

Bobby's lyrics were maladroit. One tune was about bombing the city of Los Angeles after his girlfriend has an affair with an FBI agent.

"That just doesn't sound like you. You're a great piano player, and you've got great songs. Why don't you and Leo do your own band?"

"We sold out of Hunter Thompson T-shirts tonight," I said.

Which is another rule. When a band sells out of merch, they're most ripe to break up over email.

The sixty-eight-year-old son of a sod house hay farmer grappled for the right words to say about his national television show's cancellation.

"Naturally, I'm very, very disappointed both for my Musical Family and for our television audience, too. I believe there is such a place, maybe even a need for a program such as ours."

Welk sipped his tonic water and blacked out or something. It's all written down somewhere. His aides revived him, made a few jokes about pink slips, then at his resort's nightly dinner party, he made a one-off about washing the dishes.

He had been atop network television for sixteen years. Even his doctor said his hectic pace would result in an early demise. But Welk didn't know how to stop. Some pioneer work ethic deep in his bones. He couldn't quit—it was all he knew.

By midweek, I had fielded multiple phone calls from Poncho. He wanted a California tour over winter break. But I refused, pacing around 123 Forest.

"I've got work for *South Dakota Magazine*."

Friday morning, I received an email from Bobby.

"We have an opportunity to make $300 this Saturday night at Maya Jane's."

Leo and I, however, had recording time booked.

"Can't do it, man. Leo and I are busy this weekend with our other band."

Bobby's response came fast.

"It's one thing that you can't play a winter tour. If you can't commit to a simple show in Vermillion, then we'll replace you."

So I quit.

"Good luck finding a songwriter half as good as me," I typed.

Then, feeling bad, I ran back and wrote a response that Welk would've approved of.

"We've had a good run," I said, "But we'll be happier apart."

Monster later told me: "You should've stuck with the first email."

Lawrence was too young to retire.

Within hours, he knew his next adventure: "We were inundated with mail, and we received so many requests from television stations across the nation to go on with our program that we decided to go into syndication, and in less than a week we were booked solidly from coast to coast."

The book ends with customary dopiness: Lawrence fixed himself a bowl of tapioca pudding and reflected on his roots stumbling around with a push-button out in the barn. He contemplated a timeline of how long it would take to thank everyone who helped him along his journey. He doesn't reach a conclusive number. But he dies in 1992. My bet is he sated the gratitude market sometime during

Reagan's second term. By our estimates, after thanking his family, staff, ABC staffers, the Dodge Dart marketing director, that choir director form Strasburg, maybe an odd Nebraska priest, the fans, the collective efforts of television, Technicolor engineers, and maybe a Yankton doctor, Lawrence's gratitude campaign ended in 1986. But that's a number even ardent Welkian scholars still fiercely contest.

———

Bobby updated the MySpace page to say, "Female Piano Player Needed!" Fortunately, no one joined. The Brickhouse Boys was over.

For the next month, Leo watched as our MySpace views stayed high: "Five hundred last night, did you see? More than the Throwback!"

But eventually, like everything, it faded off.

One night about a week after we'd broken up, I texted Donny.

"Can I come pick up my amp?"

"It's in the garage. Unlocked. Pick up whenever."

I trudged over to their house, snow covering the sidewalks. Only one light was on. I creaked through the garage door, grabbed my amp from the S.S. *Bly*, looking like she'd been ridden hard and put away wet, and walked back out the garage, lugging the forty-pound amp down the streets.

"Jesus . . . Heavy . . ." I panted.

My body overheated. I removed my hat and mittens. Then his familiar face came around a corner, sliding on the snow, as the tires spun friction-less.

"It's Chris from the Brick Boys!" said Monster, returning from downtown.

"Can't talk right now, Monster."

Monster kicked up snowflakes when he braked.

"Bobby's all in on the Throwback now."

"How are they taking it?"

"It's shame, man. I'm taking a bath the other night and 'There Goes My Wow' comes on my iPod, and I started tearing up. Beautiful song. But, Chris, we were playing PBS. I mean, come on. Nothing's rock n' roll about a pledge drive."

He told me to come drink with him downtown, then biked off, a tire trail following him in the snow. I walked to my apartment on Forest Avenue alone. It was penance. Not a single car offered to help. And that's a shame because you can learn a lot from the guy hauling an amp down the street.

Our *No Cover, No Minimum* episode aired in January. I went to Collette's apartment to watch the broadcast.

"Is your brother coming over?"

"Nah, he's writing music in the practice room."

No Cover, No Minimum looked like a local show. The graphics were blocky blue, with black and orange lettering in dim lighting. I wanted to narrate the events. But the show moved too fast. After a song or two, Collette laughed about something else, leaving me to stare at the television, and pick out things I hoped others would notice.

Donny texted: "Hey, I caught the show tonight at a bar television. Wish we were still out there doing it."

I wasn't sure how to respond.

Collette walked back in the room, holding a glass of wine in her hand and gave me a hug. "You sound so intelligent," she said, leaning into me, her arm around me. "Like a real musician."

CHAPTER 32

THE HIGHWAYS OF LOS ANGELES, CALIFORNIA

SATURDAY, APRIL 2, 2016

I stepped into the Pacific Ocean for the first time after driving west from Los Angeles on Wilshire Boulevard past the high, cotton-ball palm trees of Beverly Hills, into the pastel-colored strip-mall waste-land of Santa Monica, then finally to the Navy Street pier, and, I think, saw why Lawrence Welk would've loved California. There's nowhere left to go. You're on the edge of America, far from North Dakota. The sun tells you you've made it, even if you haven't.

"The Aragon was built right out on the pier so you could hear the roar of the waves as they rushed in and slapped at the pilings underneath."

I stood at the sandy lot north of Venice Beach where the Aragon Ballroom stood and tried to imagine.

The last time in *Wunnerful, Wunnerful* that Lawrence visited Stras-burg came on a "bright fall day."

Christine was at the store, so Ludwig broke out the bottle of schnapps.

"*Gesundheit.*"

Ludwig sat in bed, his wool socks floppy at the ends.

"I have been so lucky," Ludwig said. "A fine wife. Such good children. To live in this country. You know I could still beat you."

He smiled, referring to their accordion skills, a prized family trait inherited from that mythical, sightless troubadour wandering Europe a century prior.

"I'm sure you could, Father," Lawrence replied.

"You were so stubborn," Ludwig said, "The most stubborn boy. You surprised me. But I think I knew when you came home from the Hague dance that you really meant what you said about leaving. I knew you'd never stay on the farm after that."

Lawrence protested strongly.

"I knew the music was inside you that night," Ludwig continued. "I just prayed you could have your music *and* still keep your faith."

As I stood where the Aragon Ballroom had once stood, there was merely a sandy lot littered with vagabonds and drifters. A man with an unbuttoned flowering shirt revealing a big belly and a guitar next to him slept the morning away. A sign posted read, "End." Another: "Road Closed."

I had one more stop.

When I arrived at the Catholic cemetery in Culver City, situated on a pastoral green knoll separate from the hustle of Los Angeles' winding interstate highway system, I walked into the cemetery office.

"Welk?" the man asked, not recognizing.

He typed the name into the computer system.

"Related to *Fern* Welk?"

"Yes," I said, figuring Fern was listed as the most recent decedent.

He scribbled onto a map the location of Welk's grave. It was close. I folded it into my brown coat and walked out into the brilliant southern California afternoon. At the adjacent flower shop, I purchased a rose.

"Do you have pink?"

The older woman watering the plants in the shop smiled.

"My favorite, too."

I walked dozens of rows of graves—mostly Hispanic surnames giving way to the older names: Italians, Irish, German. Near the "X," I saw a mound of pink and white flowers. My heart skipped a beat. *This was it.* I walked up and peered down:

"Schmitt."

What the hell?

I spied my map again and realized I was two rows over. I walked in my cross trainers on the crunchy grass and noticed the grafted image of a man waving a baton from a few feet away. A single red rose lay lengthwise across the simple stone.

Lawrence Welk: 1903–1992.

Next to his Fern.

Music notes ran widthwise across the stone. At its bottom, his message: "Always keep a song in your heart."

Was I a fan? A protégé? What should I say?

I folded a small note carrying the words "with admiration, from a relative of Edna Stoner's in Beresford, South Dakota," and tucked the message under the stem of the flower atop the granite square.

Then I got up, smelled the lush spring air, the greenest I'd seen since arriving in California the day before, and walked to my car, wondering who else had left a flower, before retaking the maintenance road and the highway, a crush of traffic swallowing me up like a synchronized dancer against my will, as I drove, or floated, back into the city.

CHAPTER 33

GARRYOWEN, SOUTH DAKOTA, JUST WEST OF THE IOWA BORDER

APRIL 22, 1931

On our last Christmas together, Grandma McGill leaned over in a cardigan, a glitzy snowman broach fastidiously pinned, and told me a story few in the family heard.

"You knew Ed tried out for Welk's orchestra?"

The poplars would've been swelling in August, a bloated pig corpse rotting on the highway. Ed would've borrowed a Studebaker from his cousin, cantering over the gravel road down to Vermillion. His hands gripped the steering wheel, popping the veins on his hands, as the road rattled the automobile's chassis.

At the Akron Corner, the pink road ran west into Vermillion. Another thirty miles on U.S. 50, the river. Another thirty, the reservation. Another sixty, the first stone thumbs of the Badlands. Then, mountains. Faces in stone being carved.

Grass reached the sky. The driver sang.

O Danny boy, the pipes, the pipes, are ca-al-ling.

His car ambled past a windmill and into the dirt lot to the west of the college.

Ed came right home from Creighton when his mom's family lost the farm, but now he worried he might never leave.

At Carey's, pickups backed up. The tryouts were maybe announced on WNAX. Men stood in line. The orchestra at least was a job. Pulling up, Ed saw regulars Cal, Tuck, that slick-haired Alvin from Sioux City. They'd drank one night, polished off a bottle they'd then chucked into a corncrib.

A man in white shirt, brown pants, and red suspenders held up his big hand.

"Gentlemen," he said, "We will begin shortly."

Ed hadn't told Delia about the tryout.

"Christ on Sale," called out a guy, "McGill's here. Does he think it's a beauty contest?"

Everyone laughed, except Sioux City.

The line slackened. Dust rose into the summer air. Down at Carey's, men walked out—some heliotrope-faced from embarrassment. Mullen walked out and went straight to the bar across the street—Leo's.

"Next!" he called and made a jabbing motion.

Ed entered the bar, spotting a small table and chair near the bar pushed back. And *him*. The bandleader stood—tall, finely dressed, pacing back and forth, a bejeweled ring on his pinky finger, his hair slicked. He chatted to himself in a half-German, half-English.

The assistant jostled him.

"Name?"

Sweat perspired down his face.

"Ed McGill."

The man scratched down "McGill" on a slab of paper.

"Alright, Eddie," he said, grinning. The man missed a tooth. It's the trumpeter. "Boss, this is Eddie McGill."

The seated man turned.

"Very nice," he said, smiling, his large hands webbed together like a bird's nest, green eyes glowing. "And what will you be singing for us?"

"Wild Irish Rose," said my grandfather.

He's shorter, with a flash of white hair.

"Are you an Irish tenor?"

Ed nodded.

"Wonderful," Lawrence said. "I've been looking for one. Edmund, whenever you're ready."

<hr>

I wonder where music comes from.

Maybe for Ed, music came from a street in Galway, somehow passed its way through his grandfather, shipped across the Atlantic with his one-legged mother, her pant-leg blowing on the brig, or from a branch of a thistle stuck to his father's dress pants in northwest Iowa when he went hunting one humid afternoon, or from the dappled leg of a trouser wet from the Missouri River on a spring morn. Maybe music comes from the base of his collarbone. Or the bottom lip. Ed started to sing. Not flashy. No waving arms. His neck taut.

My wild Irish Rose,
The sweetest flower that grows!

Air exhaled from his lungs, his stomach, like a cantor reciting his prayers.

You may search everywhere,
but none can compare with my wild Irish Rose!

A song's never twice the same, at least for the good ones. My grandfather was one of the good ones.

When he finished in that empty bar, he nervously twiddled his soft, pink hands—stock boy hands, not plowman's—behind his back. He wore a suit. His only suit.

The bandleader shuffled the papers in his hands, busy-like. He remained seated. He was young, maybe ten years older than Ed, but already with a wide forehead cleared from slicked-back hair, florid eyes.

"Wonderful, Edmund, just wonderful. Please, leave your address. We leave for Kansas City in two week's time."

Ed checked the mailbox promptly after work every day. A week after the audition, a letter—initials "LW" scribbled in the appropriate top-left corner—leans in the mailbox. Ed's in the fields.

But Delia reached it first.

She read the invitation, some silliness from a German music man, the one on the radio, and her fingers tore the letter into tiny, self-defeating pieces.

When Ed returned from the store where he clerked, he sang "Oh Danny Boys" and "Wild, Irish Roses" and "Camptown Races" in the back of a pick-up his cousins drive. He checked and saw an empty mailbox.

"No mail for me, Mom?"

"Nope," Delia said.

This continued for another week. After two, Ed stopped looking.

Ed would never leave South Dakota. At thirty-two, he met Dolores. They danced at the Ritz Ballroom, with its trellis siding and back-bar serving bubblegum and popcorn and bits of chocolate and weak beer, and soon there's a Monday morning church wedding and later, ten children. Delia lived with them. Ed owned a grocery store, then a café. When those failed, he sold seed or pepper door-to-door for the Watkins people. He sang elegies at funerals and cut dry, dark jokes, asking, "Did he die of anything serious?" when the Johnson bachelor turned up dead. When his sons went out drinking or his daughter climbed a tree, he warned, "They'll bury you on a Tuesday."

On Friday nights, he watched the fights. On Saturday, the family gathered around couches, wicker chairs—Delores in the kitchen popping popcorn on the stove while Delia cut images of happy couples from the catalogs with her large scissors. But on Christmas Eve in 1955, Ed saw the Lennon Sisters—quadruples of organ-piping height and misty complexion. The old fire was back. He gripped the handrail of his rocking chair and went to bed early, waking in the morning to boil water, the steam in plumes enclosing the hard lines of his face, waiting to poach an egg.

He woke his daughters and drove to a recording studio in Sioux City. Rosemary, the eldest, wore a blue dress with a black bow. So did Patricia, less than a year younger. Franie and Kay (who has the strawberry-blonde hair) wore matching red dresses down to their knees. They sang like birds into a microphone. Ed in a suit stood next to the sound engineer behind a wall of glass, smiled. He had a professional photograph taken and slipped into an envelope along with a pink acetate 45 inscribed with "E. McGill" in the top left corner and "ABC Studios, Hollywood" in the center.

Maybe that's when the letter arrived. Maybe that's the letter Delia tore up. Aunt Pat told me the story. Aunt Rosemary concurred. When I asked Aunt Franie, she dismissed it. "That wasn't me. That was Rosemary. Not me."

People always said, "You're so much better than that Joe Feeney, Ed. Did you ever think about going into show business?"

Ed would smile, the knuckles on his tightening fist turning white, then doff his cap and walk out from church onto the crunchy, purple gravel that the state dug up from the quartzite quarries along the Big Sioux River and quietly drive back to his wife, his mother, and his children.

On an October morning in 1981, when Dolores returned from her morning shift, making breakfast and cleaning sheets out at Bethesda, she drove home to find Ed's car still in the driveway. Before entering the breezeway, she already knew. At the kitchen table, when she'd enter the home, she'd find him, with the morning's *Argus Leader* spread out before him, his coffee still warm, her husband's handsome, silver head lay face down on the table.

Ed was buried on a Tuesday.

CHAPTER 34

GRAND FALLS CASINO NEAR LARCHWOOD, IOWA

SEPTEMBER 3, 2016

On a Saturday night, Mom and I and Altman went to see the Lennon Sisters at the Larchwood Casino in northwest Iowa.

I got to the casino earlier, and Aunt Pat sat with her husband, Bill, near the doorway.

"Go find Cheryl, near the ticket booth. She has a surprise for you."

"Christopher?" a woman in a suit-jacket asked. "Follow me. They're just taking the last ones in."

Before I knew it, I stood in line to see the Lennon Sisters.

In the Lennons' memoir, *Same Song, Different Voices*, they acknowledge an oddness in their relationship with Lawrence Welk. They said he could on-a-dime shift to being domineering or manipulative. They feared him. But they also had memories of sitting on his lap, almost like his grandchildren, singing songs or listening to him tell stories about the farm. Plus, they must've made up, because for years they toured through the 1980s and '90s on the Lawrence Welk circuit in Branson, Missouri.

Anyway, the whole thing had the feeling of Lourdes: me and about forty-five women, many elderly, some infirm. I thought of Edna. They all gabbed amongst each other about their fandom of the Lennons. *But what was I? A journalist? A fan? An interloper?* Before I could decide, I was escorted down a concrete paved alleyway underneath the casino and ushered through a black curtain, where three women in sequined dresses, all about up to my chest in height, smiled at me.

"Why hello!?" cried Peggy Lennon.

"Hello!"

I wore a seersucker jacket and a faded blue Library of Congress baseball cap.

"I'm writing a book!"

"We've heard," said Kathy.

"Really?" I said, then wondered if they thought I was the other guy, the history professor from Indiana who was writing a serious history piece on Welk.

"Oh, well, let's . . ."

They tried strong-arming me next to them like Ralphie in *The Christmas Story.* But I planted my legs sternly and pushed out my question.

"I just have one question," I said, wondering if perhaps I should bring up Edna, other women, or what they said in their wonderful memoir, in which they talk about the "two sides" of Lawrence Welk, about his Jekyl and Hyde tendencies, but because I was never a good journalist, I flagged.

"I visited the Palladium Theater this spring in Hollywood. Do you remember singing there?"

I wanted to make them feel at home, here in South Dakota. I wanted to know what the acoustics were like. How the sound felt to them. And I wanted to mention a place they might feel comfortable at.

"The Palladium Theater," Peggy said. "Well, gosh, that's a place I haven't thought of in awhile. We actually *do* have some photographs up there, though."

"Okay," I said. "Great!"

She was trying to get rid of me. I turned to leave, but a hand caught my arm.

It was Mimi, the youngest one, the one who hadn't been an official member of the group till later.

"Thanks for saying that," said Mimi, her eyes smiling, "That
place was like home for us. It's good to think of those places when
we're on the road."

I nodded and turned out into the open ballroom, named for a
special kind of tree (Larchwood) that grows only in the prairie.

We watched the show. The Lennons were terrific. They still belt the
hits. They were so good I started to wonder if maybe they actually
regretted teaming up with Lawrence Welk. What if they'd branded
themselves in some other way? What if they had gone for a more
avant-garde approach? Perhaps moved to Manhattan and met up
with people hanging out in the Chelsea Hotel? What if they hadn't
side-carred to Andy Williams?

After the show, Mom drove back home the two hours to Wells.
Altman and I got a drink at the bar, and I spotted the pianist at a
craps table, wearing a Disney T-shirt, drinking a beer.

He was a young man, slightly balding.

"You're not the musician for tonight, were you?" I asked.

"I am," he said, looking up. "Did you see the show? You seem a
little young."

"I did. Loved it. You changed out of costume pretty quick."

"You like being on the road?" Altman asked.

He shrugged.

"See, the nice thing about these gigs," he said. "They start early,
so I usually have time to get dinner before the grillers are closed."

After finishing up our beers, we buttoned up our coats and went
out the doors. I waved goodbye to Altman in the windblown parking
lot, the darkness overriding, save for a large, digital billboard illuminating the massive faces of the Lennon sisters over the roadway,
next to this casino now in the same place that *used-ta-be* a homestead, the basis for Rolvaag's *Giants in the Earth*, and before that
used-ta-be a hunting field, a stopping-off place, a meadow.

CHAPTER 35

OUR CARRIAGE HOUSE IN
WASHINGTON D.C.

SUNDAY, JULY 4, 2020

I have a strange habit of finding bands in parks.

In the summer before the pandemic, before that wretched fence was up, I went for a jog around the U.S. Capitol and heard a strain of music flying up the hill. There, beneath the dome's feet, a military band played a free concert to a small crowd of people. So I wiped the sweat away from my forehead and stopped to listen.

Congress had fought that very day over whether or not to censure the words of the president, who told four women of color elected to Congress to "go back" to their home countries, even though they already were home. The debate was over whether his words were hateful or not. The rules had been suspended, shouting ensued.

Welk, too, was the child of immigrants. He didn't speak English correctly. It was a shame running through his life, at least according to his book. But he never thought that didn't make him American.

"Dreams do come true," Welk said, "Even for someone who couldn't speak English and never had a music lesson or much of an education."[1]

"Dreams" is the other word, next to "swizzle sticks," that shows up throughout Welk's book. "Dreams" were what awaited you at the end of a song, a television show, or a book.

---

1. Quoted one night on NPR's *All Things Considered* by Andrea Seabrooke.

Outside the Capitol, mosquitos hovered over a reflecting pool as the group played "Continental Soldier."

Usually, that insipid little tune—"Do Your Ears Hang Low" etcetera—tinny-rattles out of the ice cream trucks zooming around the National Mall. But from the wooden reeds and brass largess of this proud, little band, I wondered if a nation fell silent in heartache, or if it was maybe just catching its breath.

<hr />

One night, when Carrie and I lived in Sioux Falls, we walked a block over into the Washington Pavilion. It *used-ta-be* a high school. Now it's a performing arts hall.

The symphony did Ravel's "Bolero."

We watched the opening snare line and saw the backs of ears—small, fleshy treble clefs—bent in curious reception.

As a musician, I've not thought enough about ears. Lately I'm wearing earplugs washing dishes. It's not the sharp clank of forks on porcelain basin. It's the invisible reverberations—tiny and extreme—hitting my ear afterward.

woop. Woop. WOOP.

I worry someday, grey and whiskered, my ears will give out. Chalk it up to years of dive bar shows with tall, black speakers.

But watching the Basque ode, I remembered that audiologists say it's the brain (or maybe the heart), not ears, that do your listening. The ears are a little bowl into which the sounds spill, into which information swirls. But it's the mind, the memory of past sounds that knows how to make sense of these small data packets.

As "Bolero" rose from a small, shiny idea, the bandolier walking into the coliseum, lifting himself off the dirt, fixing his red cape, it struck me that we here in Sioux Falls were not listening to Lawrence Welk.

"Bolero" was authored in 1928 after Ravel had toured America. When he came back, his patrons needed a new song. He gave it to them. While on vacation, he played the melody on one finger at the piano and asked his friend, "Don't you think this theme has an insistent quality?"

We will hear this song for another five hundred years. The music is not to sell Geritol or to bring back memories of our grandparents. It's to swell inside us a part of the sea otherwise dormant. The music needs us. It helps us fly.

Welk was right in this way.

But we will not be listening to his music. Nor mine. But I hope that there still will be a symphony along the banks of the Big Sioux River, which runs north and then east and finally south for a hundred miles, still a nice drive from what many cartographers called the one-hundredth meridian, where the American West begins, and a whole new music, insistent and plainspoken, begins.

The cicadas buzz-sawing *see-saw-seeeeeee-sawww*.

A pickup *backfires* a hiccup.

And a young man, wandering the road, shouts at the sky, "I'm a musician! I swear, I can be a musician!"

The End

ENCORE

Lawrence Welk has a *Goodreads* page. I recently perused it and found out many things. Like, apparently, there's a book called *Lawrence Welk's Bunny Rabbit Concert* that is thirty-five pages and has one five-star review. The reviewer—assumedly British from her use of "mum"—says she's perplexed as to why she enjoyed it. Then I moved to bigger fish.

Here's what you want to know: *Wunnerful, Wunnerful* has a 3.67 rating; there are thirty-three reviews. *Same Song, Separate Voices* only has four reviews. Maybe Welk was right when he said the Lennons started "digging their own funeral" when they left his show.

Anyway, Welk's top reviewer claims the second half of the book goes by in a blur but pushes back against Germans from Russia who complain Welk didn't openly identify with his heritage enough. He says that in 1971, self-identification and/or identity politics for Germans from Russia was not yet where it is today.

So this is important.

Actually, this reviewer *does* tell us something crucial: "The self-deprecating attitudes displayed through the book can be misleading, I think. Welk continually speaks of his many foibles, his naivete, especially his ineptness at public speaking, but at the same time he brags of his successes. The self-deprecation is both a native instinct for a German-Russian boy from North Dakota and also a continuing life strategy."

Yes! Exactly! Swizzle sticks! I was happy to discover someone else thought Welk pointed out minor character flaws too exuberantly. Now we're onto something.

I continued.

Someone named "Dad" gave the book five stars. He offers a brief synopsis, telling us he "found this book in my Mom's things after she died. I decided to read it as Mr. Welk is a favorite of hers and she watched it every Saturday night. My Dad did too when he was home. My wife, Kristy's Dad and Mom were permanent watchers also. I would see some of the shows and I thought it was a good show especially the Lennon sisters, but I would never admit that to critical peers as this show was uncool for teenage boys."

Accessing inheritance through Welk rang a bell.

"Dad" wrote: "I feel able to relate better to my own mom now and others who lived through the Big Band Era."

Okay. Another reviewer who gave it a two says she snatched it from a Milwaukee giveaway day at the library. She has no idea what "blue hairs" see in him. She, bafflingly, decided to read it, though, and also comments on the smell. She makes a few cracks about bubble machines, Welk's sense of destiny, and then moves on.

They kept coming.

Kathie, who rated the book five stars, says, "I think his wife was a very patient woman raising 3 kids almost by herself."

Roo (three stars) found it mundane. She read for conversation topics with her dad. She claims to have sped read it.

And then there is Dierdra, who gave it five stars and is a woman after my own heart: "I might be an eighty-year-old in a twenty-three year-old body, but I'm okay with that!"

Situationist 45 says he'll buy up all Welk's DVDs. He gave it three stars.

And then Mel (three stars) calls it hilariously bad and says she heard Welk wasn't the easiest guy to work with.

One person didn't give any stars but said someone donated a signed copy to the thrift store she works at.

In 2011, Ryan, a budding musician, gave it five stars and said how impressed he was with all the risks Welk took.

And Leanne said Welk wasn't likeable. She gave it two stars. But said it was well written.

PASS THE HAT . . .

Fifteen miles west of Vermillion, in Gayville, South Dakota, rests Gayville Hall. It's my most not-despised venue in all of the Jim River Valley, which is less easy than you'd think. I've seen talented piano players serenade at Ben's Brewing in Yankton; a jump, jive, n' wailing band blast in the basement of the Varsity Bar in Vermillion; there's Carey's Bar, where Poker Alice plays every Friday happy hour; and I once stopped off at a former place in the road now inhabited by a sign called Pumpkin Center, where talented musicians may have gathered before the interstate—with its late night gas stations with rubbery hot dogs on rollers at all hours of the night—came through and rendered it very similar to Spink, an ambiguous pronoun of a town.

But, as I was saying, this thing called Gayville Hall exists. It's mostly an old general store that, when I was in college, was run by an eccentric Bernie Sanders-haired filmmaker who two minutes into conversation told me why he supported the socialist candidate for president in 1968—"Humphrey wasn't liberal enough for me"—but also why he couldn't bring himself to vote for Obama. Nevertheless, we agreed on music, and every Saturday night he hosted the Hay Country Jamboree, which included a fiddler who used to deejay classical music on public radio, a guitarist with an eyepatch, a woman on bass with a bob haircut, and her husband, John, the singer, who— rumor has it—used to work at the college in Springfield but now is warden at the state men's prison. The crowd was mostly geriatric. When I went to shows in college—dragging new girlfriends, kids from the newspaper—we always hurdled far below the average age for patrons. And the owner would grin and shake our hands on entrance. The acts didn't stray much from the standbys—Johnny Cash, Hank Williams I, Elvis—and the folding chairs were always filled. At intermission, they sold kettle corn and orange soda in the annex with metallic feed signs and old Coca-Cola advertisements and hundreds of pictures framing the walls. Big quilts hung on the walls, insulating the sound. And at 10 p.m., the concert ended, always with a couple of self-deprecating references to traffic or staying out late on a Saturday.

It was mostly a bizarre way to spend your twenties. Really, I leap-frogged actually making my own memories, being immersed in the gestalt of millennium hip-hop, frat parties, loud conversations over songs with machine-gun drum breaks, and instead landed in this time capsule that was slowly, like the turning of the undertaker's methodical crank, being lowered into the soft soil of the floodplain. I don't know if they knew why I showed up. But it was necessary tutelage. Some musicians demand learning a hundred covers before ever writing their own tune. I didn't learn covers. But I learned their DNA. And as an undergrad, it was like a living history museum come to life, like the snapping of the Ghost of Christmas Past's fingers in Fezziwig's hall, and all the farm lights in the Dakotas came back on, the kitchens filled with pies and mulled wine, the barns straightened up, the warped boards firm as a young ponderosa forest, the hay-stacks freshly lining the walls for insulation, and the boarded-up, busted windows and gloomy ambiguous pronoun buildings in all those small towns referencing long-lost antecedental persons and businesses now filled with lights, fresh red paint, marquees, and shopkeeps in bowties and smart hats, buttoning up coats, flipping "open" to "closed" signs, shutting down for a Saturday night, and going home to dinner before heading to the dance.

It made me happy to see this, eating my popcorn, stomping my feet to the Hay Country Jamboree, sipping my orange pop, imagining how much fuller and happier and sadder and cloistered and bustling life was in rural Dakota on the outside back when these tunes were new, back when fewer counties than now met the government's 1891 definition of "open" frontier. But I couldn't handle the letdown, the delusion's hangover, because at the end of the night, we would step out of the Gayville Hall, see the lone neon lights of a few bars down the block, and drive down the quick, black highway to Vermillion, maybe catch a drink, blow past the blackened countryside, the drained river, the massive, expensive pickups next to dilapidated buildings, and gradually decompress, come back to the real world, gain our real, non-moon weight, maybe catch a song or two of the closing metal band at Maya Jane's before walking over a dumped bowl of the nachos that the Christian students sold down-town to keep everyone from getting too drunk.

It's weird, but after the Brickhouse Boys I didn't go back to watch shows at Gayville Hall. I didn't have time for the ghosts. I'm avoid-ing them now, too. It's not that I was too busy, but the act, the gig, the historical tomfoolery and willful negation of the spilled-nacho crowd and dwindling storefronts seemed too cruel an advertise-ment. A distasteful handbill or hyperbole-infused write-up of a local garage band you know isn't true. I wasn't staying around to watch the band get back together for one song only to bury them again. Instead I stayed home.

Now if I'm driving fast on Highway 50 past Gayville on a Sat-urday night, like my Dad flying past the World's Only Corn Palace or my Mom talking quietly about Great-Grandma Delia, born be-fore statehood, whose father came from Ireland on a boat with his one-legged mother, about how he died when his hay wagon turned over on him on his way home from the fields, maybe whistling an old tune that reminded him of home, I might pull into town, drive up to the parking lot, hesitate, and then turn around, catch my breath and the highway again, because I want nothing more to do with that scene, the pasteboard sets and wagon-wheel covers, nothing more to do with imitating a past that seems unalterably private, forgot-ten, and never-to-return. Instead, I just want to visit from a distance and then leave undisturbed those ghosts dancing across the flicker-ing television screens, glowing inside the double-wide trailers and stretch-board farmhouses, which dot the lost prairie of my grand-parents' vast, syndicated dream fields.

AUF WEIDERSEHEN, 1835

At the gate this morning to Anna Kaiser's home in Prague, a blind man is sleeping. He is wrapped in scraps of clothing. A dog with sores rests near his legs, biting at the loose strings on his boots be-fore scampering off to lap up rainwater pooling in the dirt.

Anna approaches the man, blindfolded, his scraggly black hair down to his shoulders.

He is resting, she thinks, not dead.

Right beside him is a kind of bellows-box. He has traveled far. Perhaps from the east. Perhaps from the Black Sea. They will get these travelers occasionally. Men far from home. Who will come singing the old songs, who will play and then ask for some bread, whether you want them to play or not.

"Henry!" she calls back into the home.

A pot is boiling. Her husband, however, is not home. She only wanted to scare the man in case he got any ideas, in case he is not actually asleep. She doesn't want any trouble this morning. No music. No trouble. He has stopped at the wrong house if he thinks they want that.

A boy child cries in his crib.

Anna approaches the crib. A small, wooden box with lattice work on the miniature headstand, and a brown, seesaw-horse bottom.

"Georgie," she whispers. "Georgie do not cry so early in the morning."

Her other children are still asleep. Her husband is selling wares in the market.

But she will not wake them this morning with a soft song.

Sleep my little rosebud,
Sleep little dove,
Sleep for a good while,
An hour, three, four,
Baby

"Huh?"

Anna runs to the door, hearing a trickle of melody playing from the garden, the treacle-sweet of the squeezebox.

"I will chase him out with a broom," Anna thinks.

When she runs out the door and down the crooked steps, however, to the wooden gate, there is just the gate. The man in scraps of clothing with the bandana over his eyes has now moved. And she looks up and down the street, spying for his hoary head, sure his kind, like her own drunk, singing father, will certainly spring back if you give them the slightest.

ACKNOWLEDGMENTS

I took a lucky thirteen years writing this book, from the first words written at my Uncle Bill and Aunt Mary's dining room table in Minneapolis in the summer of 2008 about my breakup to my final edits emailed to the publisher in December 2021, so there are more than a few friends, family members, acquaintances, and even total strangers who offered me their two cents, an arm jab, a patient ear, or even just good humor over the years in helping me to write my "Welk book" who won't be mentioned here but were as, if not more, essential to this project as those hours in a Fargo archive. From reviewing past manuscripts, listening to me wrestle with the veracity of rumors told to me over barstools about the Champagne Music Maker, or even just offering a passing anecdote about your opinion on jam bands that, say, wound its way into chapter 7, if you see some of you reflected in these pages, know that your acts of human kindness, friendship, and literary charity have not been forgotten and will be repaid down the line by a Grain Belt or Blizzard. On that note, there were also a number of individuals who sat down with me for interviews (most memorably, Lou Ella Machin and Doris Graebner) whose comments did (or didn't) make it into my final, pared-down version, and they and their families should know that their stories, told over lemonade or a homemade meatloaf, weren't shared in vain, as they all contributed to the mental library of knowledge and homespun yarns about this man who waltzed his way into so many living rooms.

All that aside, there are some prevailing forces without whom this book would still be buried in a laptop and little more than a cocktail party schtick. First, my immediate family. My mother, Rita, and father, George, who raised me in a family of storytellers and a house of music, with sheet music strewn about and the radio on. My grandparents, Dolores and Ed McGill and George and Virginia Vondracek, who saw Welk, listened to Welk, scorned Welk, and then, at least in the early years of this book before they died, told me all they could remember about this barnstorming impresario who dilatorily showed up to the local clapboard dance halls during the Great Depression. I also want to emphatically thank my brother, Leo, who is always my first creative partner and critic and who told me, way back in Vermillion in 2008, "I like the band stuff, but I don't know about the Welk." Then there is, indispensably, Carrie Johnson, my wife, who not only accompanied me on varied Welk-related sojourns, from crumbling barns to San Diego resorts, but also provided indefatigable and feet-on-the-black-top reactions, as well as counsel, to questions profound and pedestrian, from rural life to the popularity of Gogol Bordello, and even once told me, "Don't bore people too much with your band stuff." I also want to thank Carrie's ever-encouraging parents, Drs. Dan Johnson and Mary Milroy, for allowing me to slink off to work on the book during extended holidays and sometimes even arranging an interview with a patient who knew the Polka Elvis.

Within my extended family, too, there are almost too many aunts, uncles, cousins, and second cousins to thank, but Aunt Rosemary must be atop that list for sending *Wunnerful, Wunnerful* my way. Thanks as well to Aunt Pat for filling me in on Ed's tape; Uncle Mike for reminding me not to trust everything one of his sisters tells me; Uncle Tommy for bringing up Welk at the erstwhile Truck Towne Café in Beresford over a beef commercial with a complete stranger who could validate some of the sundry rumors that had been going around town the last half century; and, of course, Uncle Billy (and Aunt Mary) for helping break the seal of silence on the holiest of gossip (family gossip), as well as Shannon Towns Dake, a niece of Edna Stoner's, who has been a good ombudsman on the latter-parts of this journey. On Dad's side, similarly, I must thank Aunt Jennifer and Uncle Ted over and over for passing along some delicious Yankton-specific gossip, as well as Uncle Tom and Aunt

Kathy (and Cousin Ellie) for putting up with the Brickhouse Boys the night (morning) we landed at the cabin. Also, I want to give a shoutout to my great aunt, Marguerite, who had to skip off at the last Nebraska family reunion to go watch Welk's television show. You are all my periscope to those hearty, mysterious times before.

In life, as in writing, it's good to have generous friends, and I am so indebted, as in past projects, to my friend, Altman Studeny, who is a brilliant interpreter of the American prairie. I similarly am grateful for the troupe of students (and faculty) at Saint Mary's University of Minnesota in Winona who aided me, from 2011 to 2015, in early drafts by organizing a reading and a manuscript-sharing that helped give me eyes and ears when both were rare. There were other beta-readers, too, who stand out for their insights that have had long carbon lives, including my friend, the elegant and incisive Jahna Peloquin, the keen-eyed writer-turned-Chicago nurse, Sarah Harper, and the observant midwestern columnist Kim Ode. I also will forever thank the staff at *South Dakota Magazine*, especially Bernie and Katie Hunhoff, for providing me not just an internship, but friendship and a community-oriented approach to storytelling in towns off the highway.

The "Welk" project also, as my school loans remind me, carried me through two graduate degrees—at the University of South Dakota (USD) and nearly a decade later at Hamline University. The instructive, encouraging commentary (and initial burst of excitement) from my USD adviser, the novelist and poet Ed Allen, is still seared into my mind ("too cute!"), and memoirist Patricia Francisco in St. Paul (and sometimes at her home in Minneapolis) offered a steadying, nurturing presence when the book was on literary cinder blocks and she promised, "Your book can be about anything, but you need to decide first." There were also at least two conferences that I took an early version of the book to, and I want to thank the good-natured professor from California who saved my trip in Albuquerque (I got my money refunded, too!) and that bookstore interlocutor in Virginia (wherever she is today!), for her love of literature, big and small. I will also never forget the creative nonfiction workshop under the direction of essayist and teacher Sven Birkerts at a summer writing camp at St. Olaf when the group, mostly people my parents' age, begged of me to continue plugging away about this guy they'd been forced to watch growing up in towns with rickety signs announcing conference championships.

Lastly, I am most lately indebted to South Dakota Historical Society Press, including editor Cody Ewert for helping steer this manuscript into harbor and past director Nancy Koupal for taking a chance on a book that drives down the lanes of history, if in a torrid, champagne-fueled indie band's van.

And I cannot conclude without saying a final word for the people who found themselves prominently depicted in this book and re-acted to the manuscripts sent to them with grace, honesty, and prob-ably more than a little forgiveness (!), and who bestowed necessary creative space and oxygen for me to build my own story. What an act of human companionship that can never be repaid. To "Heather," as well as my former bandmates, while we parted under a cloud, I count myself as lucky to have known and traveled and created and lived, if briefly, in concert with each of you, whether sharing a joke under an awning after a terrible show in Sioux City or simply riding across the Dakota prairie long before I realized the land had slowly been paving its own landscape into me. I know music and memory sustain all of you, and your lives are equally, too, flowering from our time together in that funny little college town on the bluffs over the Missouri. The South Dakota writer Kathleen Norris once wrote that the parties are never over until the stories are all told. Now, like a barkeep turning off a light, or a van carrying the band driving off into the cold night, my gig, our gig too, is finally over. As Welk would say, keep a song in your heart.

FURTHER READING/LISTENING

In lieu of a bibliography, my editor asked for a reading list, a kind of play-along-at-home series of works to read or listen to as you move through (or even after you finish up) this book. There are of course a series of pieces that might be called primary sources—Lawrence Welk's autobiographies *Wunnerful, Wunnerful* (1971) and *Ah One and Ah Two* (1974), as well as *Mister Music Maker* (1958), Mary Lewis Coakley's biography of Welk—that you could dig into if you want to know the source material for my biographical sketches of Welk.

A number of additional works inspired me, providing this project with an impetus and suggesting its shape while helping me understand (or unlearn) the rules of how to engage with popular music figures in middle America, including Chuck Klosterman's *Fargo Rock City* (2001), Andrew Beaujon's *Body Piercing Saved My Life* (2006), and Willa Cather's *Song of the Lark* (1915). I have also been aided just by generally outstanding writing about music, including James Baldwin's 1957 short story, "Sonny's Blues," many of the articles that carried Sasha Frere-Jones's byline in the *New Yorker* between 2008 and 2015, the writers of *Pitchfork* and *City Pages* during that same stretch, and the inimitable Patti Smith's poetic memoir, *Just Kids* (2010).

For the gnarly task of writing *about* reading a book, I drew on everything from J. K. Rowling's *Harry Potter and the Chamber of Secrets* (1998), to Julian Barnes' fictionalized account of Dmitri Shostakovich, *The Noise of Time* (2016), to Carlos Ruiz Zafón's *The Shadow of the Wind* (2001), recommended to me by a student. For writing about two lives simultaneously, I relied on Muriel Barbery's delightful *The Elegance of the Hedgehog* (2006). If other, more coherent ways to blend narratives exist, I've yet to find them.

While words fed my typing, music carried my spirit during my writing of the book. This included—almost ritualistically for a few years—the Austin, Texas, band Spoon's *Ga Ga Ga Ga Ga*, which I vividly remember inspecting in a Fargo record shop hours before opening at the Nestor. It still helps me return to the mood of tour faster than any photograph. When I reach for other albums to remember 2007, I return to Amy Winehouse's *Back to Black*, Kanye West's *Graduation*, and *Hands* from the Raconteurs. The latter album's description in a *Rolling Stone* review as "blues power pop" got passed around our college newspaper's editorial desk between Bobby and me like the latest dispatch from the underground. Some songs and albums woke me to new soundscapes in those early days of the band, including Elliott Smith's "Waltz #2," Beirut's *Gulag Orkestar* and *Flying Club Cup* (burned onto that CD gifted by my friend before driving to New Mexico), and—of course—the first three tracks off Radiohead's *In Rainbows*. These shouldn't be mistaken as my favorite artists; they were simply the tunes on the jukebox when I hung out in that emotional dive bar that was the Brickhouse Boys.

As for music that helped power me through writing (though I eventually settled on writing in silence), I drew strength from James Blake's *Overgrown* (2013), Frank Ocean's "Super Rich Kids," (2012), Dave Brubeck's "Blue Rondo a la Turk" (1959), and in bleaker moments, Handel's *Messiah* (1741). I also admit that I even compiled a "Champagne" playlist on Spotify at one point that expressed the essence of Welk's upbeat, cheery, and soul-spritzing musical moods, including Ricky Nelson's "Fools Rush In" (1963), Todd Rundgren's "I Saw the Light" (1972), Tennis's "Origins" (2013), k.d. lang's "Miss Chatelaine" (1992), and a song from my brother's solo project, Joey Joey Michaels, called "Different Attitudes" (2020).

If you're going to listen to one Welk song, don't make it Welk's version of "Frosty the Snowman," which invokes a dystopian flare. Instead, make it "Calcutta," which—Altman was right—will brighten up any drubbing of the home baseball team.

Finally, here's a brief list of writing haunts for this book and associated years:

- The T.A. lounge of the English Department in Vermillion, S.Dak. (2008–2009)
- An apartment above a bike shop in Rochester, Minn. (2009–2010)
- Blue Heron Coffeehouse in Winona, Minn. (2011–2013)
- Urban Bean in Minneapolis, Minn. (2013–2015)
- Haskett's Delicatessen in Sioux Falls, S.Dak. (2016–2017)
- A House off of Mount Rushmore Road in Rapid City, S.Dak. (2018)
- The Senate Press Gallery in Washington, D.C. (a few weeks in 2019)
- Our Little Carriage House on the Hill, D.C. (during the pandemic, 2020–2021)